Gifted Myths

An Easy-to-Read Guide to Myths on the Gifted and Twice-Exceptional

By Kathleen Humble

GHF Press
Lexington, MA

Published by GHF Press
A Division of GHF: Gifted Homeschoolers Forum
280 Woburn Street
Lexington, MA 02420
ghfpress@ghflearners.org

ISBN-13: 978-0692174975 (GHF Press)
ISBN-10: 0692174974

Cover design by Dickson Payne, Internal Flux
www.internalflux.com • internalflux@email.com

This book is dedicated to gifted and 2e parents and kids trying to make the chaos work.

Advance Praise for Gifted Myths

Never have I encountered a more simple, elegant and warmly accessible breakdown of the myriad myths that continue to plague the gifted community. From discerning the differences between IQ tests and achievement tests to taking on the well-meaning (but incredibly problematic) assertion that "all children are gifted," Kathleen Humble leaves little doubt that this population deserves special consideration — and that their parents deserve support, encouragement and resources. (Yes, she thoughtfully includes several of those as well.)

- **Pamela Price**, author of *Gifted, Bullied, Resilient: A Brief Guide for Smart Families* (GHF Press, 2015)

"With quiet grace, Kathleen breaks down the myths that the gifted community faces. By shining a spotlight on the different kinds of myths, the gifted, educational, and neuropsychological communities can take a long, hard look at what is falsely believed and how to advance past it."

- **Jen Torbeck Merrill**, *If This is a Gift, Can I Send it Back?*

I love how Kathleen Humble has organized her book around the myths that have created so much misunderstanding for so long about what giftedness is and how gifted children can be identified and educated. Her writing is clear and engaging. Her personal examples and quotes from other parents add credibility and readability. Her reasoning is reliable. This book is a succinct guide for educators, parents, and anyone interested in creating a better world for gifted children and for all of us.

Paula Prober, M.S., psychotherapist and author of *Your Rainforest Mind: A Guide to the Well-Being of Gifted Adults and Youth*

Also from GHF Press

Forging Paths: Beyond Traditional Schooling

If This is a Gift, Can I Send it Back?:
Surviving in the Land of the Gifted and Twice Exceptional

Educating Your Gifted Child:
How One Public School Teacher Embraced Homeschooling

Self-Directed Learning: Documentation and Life Stories

Gifted, Bullied, Resilient: A Brief Guide for Smart Families

Micro-Schools: Creating Personalized Learning on a Budget

Your Rainforest Mind:
A Guide to the Well-Being of Gifted Adults and Youth

From Home Education to Higher Education: A Guide for Recruiting,
Assessing, and Supporting Homeschooled Applicants

Boost: 12 Effective Ways to Lift Up Our Twice-Exceptional Children

Coming Soon from GHF Press
http://www.ghflearners.org/ghf-press/

Gifted Women: The Essential Guide Throughout the Lifespan
by Dr. Christine Winterbrook and Abby Winterbrook

Contents

Introduction

I remember the look on my husband's face when we realized that our son was different—that mixed look of awe and horror that makes the eyeballs bulge out in a slightly unhealthy way. A look that said, "And what do we do now?"

I had spent all day making my two-year-old son's birthday cake. Family and friends had just finished lugging all the platters and balloons into the small hall we had hired. My son, clutching at his dad's shirt excitedly pointed up at the green and white sign over the door. "EXIT!" he said rather loudly. A fluke, right?

Over the next few days, my husband and I, both puzzled, had determined that no, it was no fluke.

Now, what were we supposed to do? All our cultural touch stones of what children should do were overturned. Five months later, he was writing and putting together his own mini-sentences, and we were well and truly lost. This was not "normal," or even "just a little not-normal." We had, it seemed, stumbled into the land of bad made-for-TV movies on "genius" children, of lurid front-page spreads from the likes of the Daily Mail.

This was not what we signed up for when my husband had suggested one tipsy night that "it might be good to have some kids someday."

What started with gasps from old ladies in the supermarket aisles soon morphed into mini-lectures from complete strangers on how "they never used flash cards with their kids," while I desperately tried to stop my son reading the graffiti on the nearby playground equipment.

At our playgroup meetups, I soon found myself unable to talk about what my son was doing without feeling that the other, genuinely lovely and kind parents felt saddened about their own children.

What was happening?

Feeling more than a little desperate, I booked my son to see his first psychologist. (Yes, there would be more, three in total, plus occupational therapists, pediatric neurologists, physiotherapists, podiatrists, speech therapists, play therapists, and on and on and on.)

The slightly grizzled psychologist was calm as he walked me through the results. My son was gifted. And not just gifted, but exceptionally to profoundly gifted. I cried.

I did not want to be a tiger mum or a pushy parent. I did not want to have a child for whom school would always be an awkward fit. I did not want a Doogie Howser. In those moments, I relived my own childhood, and recalled my cousin's struggles and my husband's bad experiences. I did not want that for my ball of energy and cute smiles.

I can tell you truthfully, I knew nothing. Just like pretty much everyone else. And I had an awful lot of baggage to unpack about what gifted looked like, what it meant, and how best to help my gifted child.

I must admit, I, too, thought gifted people were all Nobel Prize winners, or created their own internet companies despite being slightly socially awkward. Or they were kids with rich, pushy parents, who had an easy ride to a top-notch school.

But those stereotypes were not my boy. Instead, he gleefully spent hours creating train maps, loved eating pancake batter, struggled to climb, had a smile which lit the room, and loved snuggling up and listening to me read him a book. Something did not add up.

And that disconnect is what started my journey to figure out where all these stories about giftedness came from. Where did these ideas start? And why does almost everyone get it so wrong?

I uncovered the strange and counterintuitive history of giftedness, where science and myth clash and combine. Turns out, the "truths" I thought I knew about giftedness were more myth than reality.

Once I started to understand not just the myths, but the history behind them, it all started to make a lot more sense. In discovering the myths and where they came from, I started to understand exactly why my family had made so many other parents uncomfortable. The bewildering feeling of having walked into an alternate world started to fade. There was sense in the madness, which was a good thing to think about on those sleepless nights when I felt everything careening out of control.

A number of myths came up again and again. Mostly, they fell into three broad categories:

- Myths based on bad, often old, research, since refuted, but lingering like a bad smell
- Straight up tall tales mixed with the occasional anecdote that caught some journalist's eye back in the day
- Deliberate falsehood, usually for ideological reasons, which not only ignored the facts, but often twisted them to suit some specific purpose

In this book, I will talk about some of the more persistent myths which fall into the above categories. Each chapter will explain what the science currently says and how the myths differ from reality.

I will also be adding the personal experiences from a survey of more than a dozen families and individuals who volunteered to write about their experiences of being gifted.

Finally, I will talk about how we can work to move away from not just believing in these myths, but toward helping individuals and in-stitutions find a way to dismantle the structures that have built up in response to these myths.

So, let's get started, shall we?

CHAPTER 1

Characteristics and Challenges of Giftedness

By the time my son was four years old, I thought I had a pretty fair handle on this gifted business. And then my daughter arrived. Where my son did not like to be held, my daughter needed to be carried everywhere. Where my son was reading and writing before his third birthday, my daughter at five had not progressed much beyond letter recognition, instead devoting hours to painting, crafting, and art. As a toddler, my son insisted that I read him books all day, and I had to put a limit on the amount I would read at a time (ten books, as I was developing laryngitis). My daughter liked one book at bedtime but developed her own rich fantasy world with many characters, friends, and a fiendishly complicated stuffed animal genealogy. My two are gifted, yet so different.

Myth: All Gifted Kids Are the Same

When you have met one gifted child, you have—wait for it— met one gifted child. Gifted children can be gifted in a variety of ways—musically, mathematically, linguistically, creatively—each with their own mix of abilities. Even their brains are wired differently. Mathematically gifted children's brains are not the same as creatively or linguistically gifted children's.[1] But whether the belief is that gifted children are all-round, high-scoring, socially and physically adept Adonises or flawed and socially awkward geniuses, or some mix of a pick-your-myth bonanza of assumptions, the emphasis remains on gifted children all being the same.

Because of the small percentage of gifted kids, creators of school gifted programs find it easier to lump them all together. But poorly thought-out programs create problems: A program that focuses on science and math might leave the linguistically or creatively gifted children out in the cold. Additionally, school programs that designate children as either gifted or disabled will not work for students with moderate to severe deficits combined with extremely accelerated abilities (also known as "twice-exceptionality"). Gifted children come in all different variations, and often what works for one gifted child with their particular mix of abilities will not always work for another. There is no universal program, curriculum, or path for gifted children.

What is Gifted?

If gifted kids are all different, do they have anything in common? An awful lot of research has been done on just this, and the consensus is that they certainly do!

The first thing to understand is that the word "gifted" describes four distinct and different groups. Researchers in education, psychology, and neurology all use the term "gifted," but they each describe different, slightly overlapping populations: educationally gifted, psychologically gifted, neurologically gifted, and twice-exceptional. When discussing giftedness, it's important to figure out which definition is being used. Otherwise, it gets confusing fast.

Educationally Gifted

People are probably most familiar with this group. These are high achievers, who score in the top 10 percent in school. When a teacher is talking gifted, they're usually referring to this group. These children do not necessarily have a high IQ. In fact, other literature may refer to them as bright, rather than gifted. Education researchers mainly focus on this group, so teachers generally only learn about this group.

Psychologically Gifted

This group scores in the top 2 percent on IQ tests (which are not the same as achievement tests) and come with a set of behaviors, abilities, and risk factors quite different from the Educationally Gifted group. The Psychologically Gifted are not necessarily high achieving. Psychologists focus on this group, mostly with smaller case studies.

Neurologically Gifted

These children fit into both Educationally and Psychologically Gifted categories, scoring high on IQ tests and in school. This is probably the best researched group of gifted children, which is a blessing and a curse. Neurologists love this group, focusing most brain studies and longitudinal studies on them.

Twice-Exceptional (2e)

These children are both gifted and have a disability, either physical, neurological, or a combination. Usually the psychological or neurological definition of gifted is used with these children, as they have already gone through a battery of psychological testing to get their disability diagnosed, but not always. Only recently has this group been recognized!

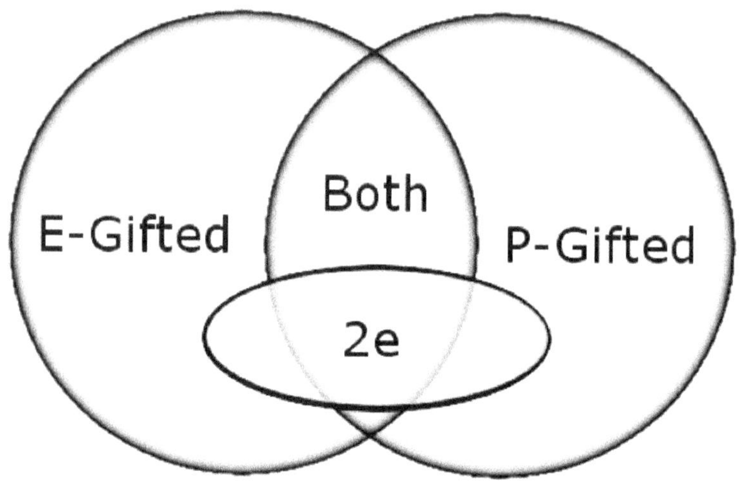

Figure 1: Types of Gifted	
E-Gifted	Educationally Gifted
P-Gifted	Psychologically Gifted
Both	Neurologically Gifted

How Does an IQ Test Differ From an Achievement Test?

If giftedness based on achievement differs from giftedness based on IQ, how does an IQ test differ from an achievement test or high grade?

For a start, an IQ test provides a clinical, medical definition. Unlike, say a spelling test, where if you get eight out of ten words right, you get 80 percent, an IQ test ranks you against others. For example, if you receive the middle score of 100, that means half the people tested answered more questions correctly than you, and half did not. That middle score is called the "norm."

When enough people do pretty much any test, something interesting happens: the range of scores follows a pattern. By plotting all those results on a graph, we see the shape of a bell emerge, imaginatively called "the bell curve." One really good way to outline the shape of the bell is to measure something called the "standard deviation," which is a quick and easy way to show how far someone's score is from the middle score, or "norm."

This is where it gets cool. Take one standard deviation step away from the middle, and that covers about 34 percent of all the scores people get. Add that up for both sides of the middle score, and we get about 68 percent of people. Now, if we step two standard deviations away from the middle, we capture 48 percent of people on either side, which adds up to 96 percent of people. This leaves about 2 percent of people on either side who are more than two standard deviation steps from that middle value. Clinical giftedness sits on the 2 percent on the right-hand side.

A bit confusingly, this does not directly relate to IQ numbers, as every IQ test has its own way of assigning numbers to that bell-curve. Most modern tests use one hundred for the middle value and fifteen points for each standard deviation step. But in practice, this varies. For example, in some populations, the standard deviation is less than fifteen, while older tests, such as the SB-LM, still use sixteen points for each standard deviation.

To confuse the matter more, each IQ test, and there are dozens and dozens of them, tests for slightly different things. Even though most tests these days will give either an IQ number or a percentile (and the numbers all look very similar), we have no easy way to compare the results from different tests. Consider that IQ tests do not just test "smarts" (or "g," as researchers like to call it), they also test how a brain works and screen for particular disabilities.

Still, two main types of "smarts" are measured in most IQ tests: Performance IQ (PIQ), which measures math abilities, and Verbal IQ (VIQ), which measures verbal/language abilities. Each IQ test measures these differently, some valuing VIQ more, others PIQ, which is why a child tested on two or more tests (or even different versions of the same test) can receive very different results.

Now add in the Flynn Effect.

James R. Flynn discovered that over time, populations get better at taking IQ tests. If a person is tested using a ten-year-old test, they will get a result roughly three points higher than on a new test (adjusting for the country and demographic). The Flynn Effect is why IQ tests are rewritten about every ten years. The Flynn Effect also applies to gifted children.[2] In fact, the older the test, the more children who will test gifted, and the younger the test, the more children who will not. Thus, the two percent cutoff does not provide a yes/no answer, but a fuzzy "perhaps."

Looking Closer at the Triple Curve—or How Math Illiteracy Leads to Dodgy Conclusions

When looking at populations, we should end up with a nice bell shape—which we typically do. But if we look closely at IQ tests, a weird anomaly appears at each end—each side has a small cluster, or "bump," rather than the expected smooth lines. These bumps have been used as pseudoscientific proof that there are distinct types of people, much like the Alphas, Betas, and Gammas in Brave New World. People liked this idea as it agreed with their biases, despite its being questionable, and, with a little bit of math and basic statistics, very easy to pull apart.

To understand why, you have to understand how IQ tests are written. IQ tests can only test for abilities in a certain range. The questions eventually run out, after all. If a kid answers all the questions right, they gets the maximum result on that IQ test (a test ceiling), and if they get them all wrong, they get the minimum (a test floor), but that doesn't mean the number represents real ability. If the test ceiling is too low or the floor too high, clusters of people will test near the top or bottom, because the test cannot tell the difference.

To check the accuracy of an IQ test before releasing it, researchers need a lot of kids, of all ages and from a variety of backgrounds. But trying to find enough kids in the right age range at the very top and bottom creates a problem: Once we get to the really rare kids at either end, the IQ number is basically nonsense. The score a kid gets when they're outside that well-calibrated middle zone becomes somewhat random, dependent on the skill of the testing psychologist, the rapport between the child and the tester, whether the child has had enough to eat, if the child is getting tired, and on and on. One question right or wrong in these edge zones makes a huge difference in the IQ number.

In math, when random wobbles are added to each result, a graph of many results will form a bell-curve shape. So, the "triple bump" is an artifact of statistics. There are no real Alphas, Betas, and Gammas, which makes it worth our while to look at and understand bad ideas, rather than ignore them. Bad ideas tend to fall apart when we do. Science is cool like that.

Why Behavioral Characteristics Matter

For nonachievement-based definitions of giftedness in particular, pinning a hard cutoff to any score can be difficult and inaccurate, requiring more of a sliding scale. Interestingly, researchers have found that the higher the IQ score, the more likely a child will display certain behavioral traits. These behavioral and brain-wiring differences are at the core of why having a high IQ does not equate with doing well on a school test, and why the two ideas are not interchangeable.

The definition used by the Columbus Group, a group of highly re-garded researchers in giftedness, goes deep into the core of what being gifted means as a lived experience:

> *Giftedness is **asynchronous development** in which advanced cognitive abilities and heightened intensity combine to create inner experiences and awareness that are qualitatively different from the norm. This asynchrony increases with higher intellectual capacity. The uniqueness of the gifted renders them particularly vulnerable and requires modifications in parenting, teaching, and counseling in order for them to develop optimally.[3]*

Asynchronous development means that a child doesn't develop abili-ties in the same way or at the same time compared to most children. A list of developmental milestones for a three-year-old will not match the development of a gifted three-year-old, who may be spot on, behind, or way ahead depending on the milestone.

My daughter is an excellent example of this asynchrony. She was always an alert baby, raising her head and looking at me while still in the hospital. She also never slept for long. She walked at eight months and loved to create elaborate drawings and paintings, spending hours concentrating on the right mix of colors and shapes. But at four years old, she struggled with the basics of toilet training, as she did not like to pause what she was doing—the world was too amazing, and she hated missing out. All those baby books I read on typical development did not help at all!

Overexcitabilities and Openness

Dr. Kazimierz Dabrowski, a Polish researcher, created his theory of Positive Disintegration when he noticed that some people were more sensitive and reacted in more extreme ways than average, but that they also had a greater ability to do difficult tasks. We now call it Overexcitabilities (OEs), and from recent research, OEs appear in over 50 percent of gifted children and can come in different combinations and intensities.[4]

OEs were also recently found to be a subset of the Five Factor Model of Personality (FFM)[5], which measures each person using a range of five different personality traits:

- Extraversion
- Neuroticism
- Openness/Intellect (which correlates with IQ)
- Agreeableness
- Conscientiousness

When I took my kids to see a specialist, I would spend forever filling out forms on the weird things my kids do (while simultaneously trying to stop them dancing on the waiting room furniture). I really hated those forms. Naval-gazing at a catalogue of every parental misstep, naughty-child behavior, or embarrassing moment is not exactly a favorite pastime. Those forms were based on the FFM. Pretty much every screening test for disability has the FFM buried inside. We use the FFM to figure out how brain wiring relates to behavior and have found it vital in figuring out how gifted kids tick.

Although research on FFM is well established, gifted researchers have resisted using it, preferring to stick with OEs. This makes sense. The FFM is judgmental, framing personality on a "good" to "bad" scale. The disability community calls this the "medical model of disability." Not surprisingly, disabled people do not like it much either. But though the wording needs improvement, the FFM remains useful to understanding how behaviors are linked to brain differences.

The five OEs and five of the six subcategories of the FFM trait of Openness are virtually identical. The subcategories of Openness follow in bold, alongside the corresponding OE in parentheses:

Actions Trait (Psychomotor OEs)

- Kids are energetic and need to move a lot. They may, in fact, have trouble if they do not move enough during a typical day.
- This may be in the "normal" gifted range or due to something else, like Attention Deficit Hyperactivity Disorder (ADHD) and is difficult to parse clinically.
- This is the only trait with a statistically low correlation to giftedness.

Aesthetics Trait (Sensual OEs)

- Kids are extra aware of sensory input, which includes taste, touch, smell, hearing, sight, vestibular (body's location in space), and proprioceptive (balance).
- May come with a heightened appreciation of beauty.
- This may be due to giftedness or a dual diagnosis, such as Sensory Processing Disorder (SPD).

Ideas Trait (Intellectual OEs)

- Kids need to understand and consume knowledge, ask endless questions, and have a drive to find "the answer."
- Kids have strong feelings on ethical issues and can be quick to point out when adults do not live up to expectations.
- Even though they understand difficult and disturbing ideas, they may not be emotionally ready to process them and may react in age-appropriate ways. These strong reactions can make it difficult to separate whether these kids are just gifted or gifted with Autism Spectrum Disorder (ASD).

Fantasy Trait (Imaginational OEs)

- Kids tend to be "away with the pixies," as their imaginations can be far more interesting than the real world.
- They often have intense dreams and an amazing ability to create their own worlds.
- Can have problems with separating out truth from fiction as they elaborate on the sometimes rather boring real world.
- Kids with lots of creativity (and their siblings) can be at slightly higher risk for developing schizophrenia, although it does not appear until adolescence.

Feelings Trait (Emotional OEs)

- Kids are very sensitive to other people's emotions.
- Kids often experience intense feelings, which can be hard to regulate.
- Often described as empaths, these kids seem to instinctively understand the emotions in a room, which can be confusing for young kids.
- A great capacity for deep attachment to people, places, and things. These kids can be "too much": too happy, too sad, too intense, too needy.

Even though research on how giftedness fits with the FFM is new, we can already use it to screen for gifted kids by focusing on only seven subcategories of three traits: Openness, Agreeableness, and Extraversion. For example, under Openness, gifted children usually have stronger idea, fantasy, and aesthetics traits, while under Agreeableness, their modesty and tendermindedness are often less than typical. Under Extraversion, they're typically more assertive and less gregarious than nongifted children. Though this may not catch all gifted children, the kids it does find will be gifted.

By focusing on behaviors rather than IQ tests alone, we can find gifted kids who might otherwise be overlooked. It also enables us to better understand what is a natural consequence of giftedness, and what might actually indicate an underlying disability[6] in a more integrated and holistic way.

Highly to Profoundly Gifted

At the far-right end of the bell curve are the crazy-smart, scary-high IQ kids: the highly, exceptionally, and profoundly gifted.

If you have one (or more!) of these kids, you will probably have to throw away every parenting book you ever purchased. Their even more extreme brain wiring means that they do not just cover material fast, they inhale knowledge, often leaving parents completely puzzled when their child makes the leap from no knowledge to complete mastery without any visible in-between steps. These children will also be far more likely to display characteristics commonly associated with diagnoses such as ASD, ADHD, Obsessive Compulsive Disorder (OCD), anxiety, and sensory problems.

Ravi struggles with learning to harness emotions. The school told his family that gifted children have no problems and will achieve academically on their own. But Ravi prefers to do only what is required. He struggles with navigating the school system and getting the help he needs. The teachers and administrators don't understand Ravi's emotional side and point out every little behavior problem as evidence he's not gifted. When he tested as gifted, that stopped. But the teachers and administration still don't understand overexcitabilities.

Despite the fact that almost every "prodigy" style exposé focuses on these children, we know surprisingly little about them, including how to accurately identify them.

Keep in mind that IQ tests are carefully designed to represent population demographics, but only have sample sizes in the low thousands at best. When dealing with children who are one-in-a-thousand to one-in-ten-thousand, such small samples are too low to differentiate highly from profoundly gifted. Additionally, many modern tests do not have enough "head room" for gifted kids, so they often run out of questions! This is called the "test ceiling," which means the results will be less than the child's actual ability. Further, due to their cautious and meticulous attention to detail, gifted kids often have slower processing speed results, which result in large differences between IQ subtests. At present, no IQ test can accurately measure "how far" scary-smart kids are from average.

I call these kids "backward professors," able to understand exceedingly complex ideas almost instantly, but having to work backwards from that point to understand the simpler concepts. Consider the gifted child who can understand college-level mathematics but struggles with multiplication tables, or the gifted pianist who plays advanced pieces by ear but struggles to read music, or the advanced reader who tackles books and ideas years beyond peers but struggles to formulate a paragraph.

Goodbye sequence and pedagogy! Standard methods just do not work with these kids.

Gifted Brains: Looking Under the Hood

Are gifted brains really different? According to neuroscience, yes. And we can tell that using techniques like functional Magnetic Resonance Imaging (fMRI), commonly known as brain scans, which show that:

- *Gifted brains operate at a higher metabolic rate and have more neural connections* (more neurons and neural activity). This has been called "Brains on Fire."[7] This means gifted brains react more, which helps explain OEs and how they retain and access more memories due to that intensity (emotions help to imprint memories).[8] This is possible because gifted brains can dial down or turn off the bit of the brain that limits overactivity.[9] This works because their brains are highly efficient, absorb and process data quicker, and switch and connect more easily between the two brain hemispheres.[7] Wonder why your kid can just absorb everything, even the half-hearted promise you made two years ago? It's their darn brain, the vacuum cleaner of all information.

- *Those that are mathematically and musically gifted have overdeveloped right hemispheres and slightly underdeveloped language centers.* Testosterone levels in a developing fetus in the second and third trimester cause this overdevelopment.[10] People with schizophrenia, bipolar disorder, and autism also display this high testosterone/overdeveloped right hemisphere.[11] Additionally, high prenatal testosterone is also observed in left-handed people, which is why gifted people are more likely to be left-handed.[12]

- *The bit of the brain associated with working memory is far more active,* which probably contributes to the higher working memory, or "problem solving space," scores of gifted children. [13] So when a kid balks at having to "show their work," understand that they really are doing it in one massive step—all on that giant blackboard in their brain.

- *On average, gifted brains are bigger.* This is true for both white matter in the brain, which helps the flow of information, and grey matter, which process information.[14] These increases are not across the whole brain, but only found in specific parts, in the prefrontal cortex, or the "reasoning bit" of the brain.

Gifted kids really can out-reason you. The logical fallacies of the overtired parent stand no chance.

- *Gifted brains' cortexes grow differently.* In a study done on both gifted, high IQ, and average IQ children, the thickness of the cortex in gifted children developed faster, but reached its peak much later (at approximately eleven years old). In comparison, peak thickness for average-IQ children was reached at approximately seven years old. This means gifted children's brains are still growing when other children's brains are more stable. Gifted children take longer to "grow" into their adult brain.[7] Hello, asynchronous development!

Based on this, we can see that gifted brains are wired to think and grow differently. Trying to work against that wiring is unlikely to go smoothly. By understanding the ways our kids think differently we stand a much better chance of finding the places where they can be happy and thrive.

Now that we better understand what giftedness really means, let's discover how we got into the current mixed-up mess.

CHAPTER 2

Ideological Zombies

Two of the myths that I faced regularly as a parent of a gifted toddler were that "all children are gifted" and, conversely, "hard work can make you gifted." I'm still not sure exactly how these two work together or how people hold those two ideas in their heads at the same time. Maybe it went something like, "My child could have been gifted too, but I didn't use flash-cards because I'm a 'good' parent who let my child play instead"?

How exactly did these myths come about?

Myth: All Children Are Gifted

The "everyone is gifted" comes from a good place, embodying the idea that every child has the ability to be great at something. In a way, it flows from our democratic traditions of "all people are created equal."

Some of this stems from the word "gifted" itself, which sounds an awful lot like "gift." This makes the whole thing feel like a present, rather than something innate, which might have been the idea when Leta Hollingworth, an American psychologist known for her contributions to the development of intelligence theory and testing, coined the term back in the 1920s. Back then, having a higher IQ was seen as mostly positive, with no dark clouds of history hanging around. Still, though the idea may not seem too harmful, the term "gifted" mixes up a diagnostic term with normal language, causing a lot of confusion.

Unfortunately, "every child is gifted" has moved beyond an inclusive idea to one that actively impedes education and life quality. For example, when a parent or advocate explains why a child needs a different educational approach or parenting style, instead of receiving help, they're often met with "every child is gifted." This blocks parents and advocates at the first step, requiring them to convince people that gifted children are inherently different and deal with the subsequent mismatch. No wonder parents feel their requests go unheard!

Of course, part of this is because teachers are only taught about one type of gifted child: the high-achieving, educationally gifted child. As these children are defined by how well they do in school, rather than more innate qualities like behavior or wiring, the idea that every child can be high-achieving has become muddled with the idea that "every child is gifted." And for the educationally gifted, a lot of evidence shows that their high achievement is heavily influenced by environment.[15]

Remember from chapter one that only some high-achieving children have a high IQ. Many high-IQ children, if not most, are not high-achieving and won't do well without accommodations.[16] Taking teachers and administrators back to the drawing board and explaining how kids with different needs

We are hoping she stays focused in high school. Motivation is somewhat of a concern for us right now. She seems more concerned with "fitting in" which means she's not wanting to "stick out" academically. She was also very bored in her ELA [English Language Arts] class this last year but is not interested in subject acceleration. I am on the fence about addressing this with her school. I am worried she will start that slow, slippery road of underachievement. ~Gifted/2e Survey and abilities can fall under the gifted label could go a long way to meeting the needs of all gifted children in the classroom.

Myth: Hard Work Makes You Gifted

In Malcom Gladwell's bestseller, Outliers: The Story of Success, he claims that anyone can be an expert with 10,000 hours of deliberate practice—a lovely idea that has, in most cases, been taken out of context. Not everyone needs 10,000 hours to master a field. One of the more obvious examples of this is prodigies who mastered chess, some in under three years. To do this with the 10,000-hour rule, they would have needed to practice every day for more than nine hours without break from birth—very unlikely, even for a child prodigy! Since Gladwell's book came out, many scientific studies, not just on chess masters but also on elite athletes, have found little if any link beyond a basic amount of practice, between the hours practiced and a person's performance.[17]

Understandably, people find the idea that anyone can become super awesome in a field with just an awful lot of hard work very appealing. If you work hard enough, you can do anything! While you will never become super-exceptional at anything without effort, no matter how awesome you are, you are never going to be big in the NBA if you are five feet tall. For those people at the top, a small or large height, speed, or neurological advantage can make a huge difference. That's a measurable, albeit uncomfortable, truth.

Why are successful people successful? This question is at the heart of early research into gifted people. It's been used to justify services for gifted people, and to take them away as well. But, interestingly, the answer to that question may not relate to giftedness at all.

Myth: Gifted People Always End Up Running Things

Throughout history, people have been grappling with questions about why certain people do well and others don't. With the wane of class-based rule at the end of the nineteenth century and into the early twentieth century, people struggled to figure out why certain people did well.

People were also interested in figuring out a new "scientific" reason for why wealthy people ended up in positions of power.

The new wonder tool of IQ tests, a scientific and evidenced-based way to measure human capacity, seemed like a perfect way to show there was an underlying reason eminent people became eminent. Researchers, such as Lewis Terman, a pioneer in educational psychology in the early twentieth century, worked hard to try and identify people who would succeed and who embodied the idea of a perfect human. But if IQ tests measured "perfect," they could also measure "imperfect." Using these IQ tests as a justification, universities in California pioneered the idea of mass nonconsensual sterilization of disabled people. Similar programs existed for criminals, African Americans, Latinos, and Native Americans. Researchers believed they could sort people into "winners" and "losers" with one convenient, easy-to-use test.

The new tools gave people a way, that looked "scientific," of justifying why the current "order" was natural and a reason to exclude people.

But they were wrong.

The thing is, high IQ and high achievement have been conflated for so long that they're now considered synonymous, when in fact, the two aren't necessarily related at all. In fact, due to the way students are usually selected for studies, they're affected by something called Berkson's Bias.[18]

Because children with behavioral differences, low achievement, or from minority backgrounds are less likely to be picked for studies, a correlation between high achievement and high IQ has been created where it doesn't actually exist. This is also true for high achievement in school and lifetime outcomes of achievement.

Berkson's Bias kicks in when the selection criteria for entering a study exclude people who should have been included. The selection criteria create a relationship that does not actually exist, because it eliminates all the people who have one or the other condition. For example, someone with high IQ may not do well in school or life or conversely, someone may do well but not have a high IQ.

Recently, genetic studies have been able to "get around" the problems with behavioral / IQ assessment studies by going straight to the source: the genes identified with high IQ. Using these cross-population studies, they have been able to show that kids with high IQ or even kids with high achievement in school *don't* have a massive advantage in life. And high achievement in school only counted for 11 percent of the difference in life outcomes for all people.[19] For children from poor backgrounds, even the top achieving kids are less likely to graduate from university than wealthy children from the lowest achieving group.[20]

These results have largely undercut the whole reason that gifted research started: trying to find reasons why eminent people became eminent. But it also opens up a conversation for understanding how kids who have histori- cally been overlooked may have untapped potential that can help us all.

Gifted is not perfect. Gifted is not always high-achieving. Gifted doesn't give much of an advantage in life. Gifted is not *better*. And gifted kids need help to thrive and succeed.

Myth: Gifted Kids Are All Well-Adjusted High Performers

Do gifted children need help or support? Often, whether intended or not, schools tend to answer, no.

Because entry to gifted programs usually focuses on achievement tests, gifted children with special needs, from poor or underrepresented minor- ity backgrounds, or the highly to profoundly gifted—in other words, the groups of gifted children most in need of support—are simply overlooked. Teachers nominating children to test for gifted programs are usually only aware, at best, of one type of gifted student: the educationally-gifted (See chapter 1). As a result, teachers miss more than 60 percent of all gifted children in a class.[16] The stereotypical image of a gifted child is very different from the reality of a gifted child. But even if a gifted kid fits the stereotype, they still need support for the same reason as special needs kids: the methods usually used to teach in a classroom are a poor fit for how their brains need to learn.

- Gifted kids absorb new knowledge at a faster rate and typically need to see new material only one to two times to learn it. (Most children need to see material three to five times, and some children need more.)
- Highly to profoundly gifted kids don't learn material in the same order as other kids. They prefer a whole-to-part approach that starts at an abstract level before moving back to specific examples.

These learning difference pose a problem in typical classroom settings:

- Without extra or different programming, gifted kids spend a lot of classroom time waiting rather than learning. Bored, smart kids will often find ways to keep themselves occupied—often in creatively disruptive ways.
- Repeatedly going over material they already know harms gifted children. When gifted children are forced to cover material three or more times, they will often unlearn it. After being taught in a regular classroom using standard methods, they can know less than the other children, or even less than what they knew before walking into the classroom.[21]
- The spiral method of teaching (which repeats information every year) often means that gifted children learn nothing new at school for years at a time.

- Gifted kids who understand material quickly and are not intellectually challenged don't get a chance to practice study, planning, or organizational skills. This can set them up for dropping out of school or burning out in college.
- Gifted kids who're labeled with behavior problems are at greater risk of going to prison. This is particularly true for minority gifted kids.

My daughter was diagnosed as 2e when she was in second grade. For me, this diagnosis was an "aha!" time because I am an educator who could not figure out my kid. Her first school district did not think she should participate in the gifted class because they thought it would be too rigorous, fast-paced, etc. for her. Thank goodness her third grade teacher fought for her right to be there. Her fourth-grade teacher discovered that she focused more when the material was more "high level," so she got that much-needed IEP for gifted services. ~Gifted/2e Survey

CHAPTER 3

History Twists Giftedness

Over the years, many parents of gifted children experiencing problems have contacted me to ask for recommendations for psychological testing or advice on how to talk to teachers. These questions usually arise because the school or teacher isn't listening to the parents' concerns. The families represent many different ethnic and socioeconomic backgrounds—from bankers to families on public assistance. A good portion of the parents don't speak English as a first language. Often, they're told their child doesn't need extra help, or only needs help for their disability.

Consider "Tom," a child I met who lived in public housing and was being raised by a single parent. Tom was incredibly smart. In just two years, he taught himself to speak and read English with near perfect comprehension. After Tom started running away from school, school administrators decided to find out what was "wrong" by testing him—in English. The kid studying college-level biology while in early primary school tested as "mildly" gifted. Consequently, Tom was refused all acceleration, as well as access to the gifted program. His mother, despite severe financial difficulties, pulled him out to homeschool him. She felt left with little choice: no one at the school was willing to listen, and she did not have the language skills or income to fight them. As far as the school was concerned, her son was a low-income delinquent, not gifted.

Myth: Giftedness is a Social Construct (i.e., Made-Up)

When looking at most gifted programs, the children in them rarely match the demographics of the rest of their school. This begs the question: Are gifted classes really about inherent ability or does IQ just measure the wealth and education of the parents? And if the answer is the latter, does that mean that IQ is just made up? Well, that question jumps the gun a bit. First, we need to understand how kids are picked for these classes.

In experiments done in Broward County, Florida, researchers found that children from poor and/or minority backgrounds were overlooked when teachers picked whom to test for gifted programs (unless the teacher was also a member of that minority group).[22] Interestingly, when all children were given IQ tests in a school, the number of African American and Hispanic American children in gifted programs went from virtually nil to the numbers expected based on local demographics. Sadly, despite the evidence, when the IQ testing was removed for funding reasons, the number of children from these populations went back to virtually zero again. The IQ testing was not the problem; the problem was who got picked to be tested.

Gifted testing is expensive, which is why almost all programs (and quite a few research studies) try to limit the number of tests. Unfortunately, the people doing the picking (usually teachers) have no idea what gifted, gifted and disabled, poor and gifted, or gifted and culturally diverse look like. Basically, they miss gifted kids who are underachieving or have behavior problems. They miss twice-exceptional kids almost completely.[23] And regardless of high achievement, African American and Hispanic American students remain less likely to be referred for gifted testing.

As discussed in chapter 1, giftedness can be hard to spot without training. As a result, teachers and administrators often select kids for gifted programs based more on stereotypes than abilities or needs.

Children in gifted programs look alike, not because there is something fundamentally wrong with the idea of giftedness, but because selection for programs relies more on intuition, myth, and stereotypes than rigorous science.

Gifted Cubed: Genetics, IQ, and Race

When we try to answer questions about what is inherent and what is made up, we must use caution, especially when we see data that agrees with our deepest prejudices. Whether the data seems to indicate that we can classify the IQ of groups of people based on what they look like or that IQ is just made up because "rich, well-educated people always score higher," closer inspection will show us that the answer is not what we think but is usually far more interesting.

The idea that average IQ differences in different populations mean something was most recently brought to the public in the book, *The Bell Curve: Intelligence and Class Structure in American Life*, by Richard J. Herrnstein and Charles Murray. At the time of the *Bell Curve's* publication, the average IQ of African Americans was fifteen points lower than that of White Americans, which in turn was less than that of Asian Americans. Herrnstein and Murray attributed this to genetic

Jirani's parents became aware he had been overlooked for the gifted program when a fellow parent asked about an excursion to the local science museum for the gifted class. Jirani, while not the top student in his class, was well ahead of his friend Nathan who had been admitted to the program. Jirani's parents requested a meeting to talk with the school but were unable to get any answers. Instead, with the help of the local gifted organization, they formally requested testing—a mine field of paperwork. Jirani tested as moderately gifted and was only then admitted to the program. ~Gifted/2e Survey differences between these populations, in an attempt to relook at the old ideas of "master races." But science, which is rarely static, now disagrees.[24]

From current identical/fraternal twin studies, we know that while intelligence is about 80 percent inherited, no single gene codes for more than three IQ points. In China, researchers are attempting to figure out how IQ works by studying the genetics of children and families from a school for profoundly gifted children. As of yet, they have been unable to pin down any simple link between genetics and IQ.[25]

Compared to other species, our human population contains little genetic diversity. No matter how we break up groups, whether socio-economically, racially, or nationally, genetic diversity within each group is bigger than between the groups. We have a range of differences, but they're pretty much the same across all populations. Current thinking suggests that some time in prehistory most ancient humans were wiped out, leaving only a small population behind. Small populations have less genetic differences than large populations. And while random mutation over time will add that diversity back in, we are still not up to the levels of other species. This lack of diversity means that population-level genetic differences cannot account for the different average IQs between socioeconomic and cultural groups, no matter how we slice and dice the data. If you have a college degree, you are slightly more likely to have a higher IQ score than a fruit picker who didn't finish high school. But an awful lot of fruit pickers will have higher IQs than you.

But this research creates a problem. If the IQ difference is not genetic, then is it environmental? Is it something to do with the test? Is it measuring real ability differences at all? Any of these will result in overlooking kids for entry into gifted programs from groups with lower averages. How exactly do we then decide fairly who gets into the gifted program? This presents a real problem for gifted children from diverse, non-English speaking, or low-income populations, particularly if they also have a disability. Termed "gifted cubed"[26] or 3E[27], giftedness, disability, and disadvantage combine to create a perfect storm that leaves so many of these children without the support they need to succeed.

How do we find these children? Achievement testing will miss the underachieving gifted kids or the kids who started school further behind. And though fairer than letting teachers decide, IQ tests still result in differences in average IQs. We need to find gifted kids who do not test well, while finding a way around IQ differences and achievement gaps.

One way to find gifted kids from disadvantaged backgrounds is the Coolabah Dynamic Assessment, a two-stage test created to find gifted Aboriginal children in Australia.[28] First, kids take a simple test. Those who score highly are noted. Whereas most other methods stop here, the Coolabah Dynamic Assessment continues by putting the class through a remedial course, focusing on the ideas in the previous test. The class is then retested. Students who score highly on the second test or who have massive gains between their two scores are noted, and both groups are then either admitted to the gifted program or referred for further testing. Fairer than straight achievement testing, the Coolabah Dynamic Assessment acknowledges that some children have not been exposed to certain ideas before, while also testing one of the most noted characteristics of gifted kids: fast learning. It's significantly cheaper than IQ testing every child up front, and the Coolabah Dynamic Assessment is scalable for schools with limited budgets.

Myth: Lessons for Gifted Children are Just "Best Practice" Education

Unfortunately, most schools do not use dynamic testing, opting instead for the easier method of broadening the criteria for getting into gifted classes. Most schools do this by redefining gifted as the top ten percent. This standard may capture gifted African Americans, Hispanic Americans, and other minority groups from the top 2 percent, but by lowering the entry criteria, this method also catches lots of bright, but not gifted, kids from other demographics. The gifted kids, particularly the highly and profoundly gifted, often become outliers even in the gifted classes.

If the point of gifted classes is to provide gifted kids with different methods to learn best, but most of the class is not gifted, what happens? It's a real muddle, which has led to a lot of mixed up thinking in education and education research.

With no consensus between districts or within schools of what defines "high achievement," comparisons of different gifted programs and techniques become problematic. Without at least minimally administering IQ testing on the children in these classes, the results and best practices of the various programs cannot be broadened to cover gifted children who do not fit the educationally gifted mold. This results in the near impossible challenge of distinguishing clear successes from failures of gifted programs, especially when many are not truly gifted programs or designed for gifted children.

This muddled up thinking has led many in education to believe that techniques used in gifted classes should be used for all students, as it's just "best practice" education. Some even wonder why we should have a gifted class at all. And because of the previously mentioned problems in selecting children for testing, this new method of best practice education still doesn't solve the problem of finding and helping gifted kids from disadvantaged backgrounds.

By the way, if you're wondering how to tell if a gifted program is designed for high-IQ gifted kids, you only have to ask one question: Would this program work equally well with neurotypical kids? If the answer is yes, you do not have a program designed for gifted kids, but for bright, high achievers.

Myth: Gifted Kids Are Needed as Role Models
in a Mixed-Ability Classroom

Confusion over who is gifted and what that means leads to weird ideas about how best to help gifted and other children. One resultant myth is that gifted kids in a mixed-ability classroom can be used as role models or teachers for the other students.

Gifted children are no more likely to know why they think the way they do than someone with autism or any other brain difference. What they get out of a mixed-ability class is how to act "normal," in other words, how to fake it. And much like kids with disabilities, gifted kids will struggle without accommodations, though their struggle will usually show up as a lack of interest in learning or in higher dropout rates from high school or higher education. By staying in a mixed-ability class without acceleration, gifted kids never learn how to study or plan. Often, the joy of learning is sucked right out of them because they never get to *learn* in the classroom.

This muddled-up thinking about the benefits of mixed-ability classes happens because teachers often don't understand that gifted kids are just wired differently. Even those who understand that gifted kids are wired differently may believe that a gifted kid can still help other kids learn. But unless the gifted child has access to advanced teaching and social interaction techniques, that child is unlikely to be able to help other students. After all, gifted kids solve problems and learn differently from more neurotypical students. For example, gifted kids often skip steps and apply whole-to-part learning. For a gifted kid to help in the classroom, they would need to understand how other kids think and learn, then alter their explanation of the material from their way of learning to the other students'—a tall task for any kid (or indeed most adults, which is why adults get teaching degrees).

Social problems also figure into the near-guaranteed failure of this thinking. Students used as a teacher's aide can get confused about whether they're a student or a teacher, undermining their ability to relate to the other children. Children struggling to learn will not see a child who "just knows" material as a role model. Those gifted children are too different and, if confused about their role in the classroom, potentially bossy.

Teachers also struggle due to this myth. Because gifted kids learn so differently, putting them in a mixed-ability class without other supports also puts an immense burden on the teacher—one that few are trained to handle. Keep in mind that only a handful of education degrees in any country have modules on teaching gifted children, and these are usually confined to master's courses.

As decades of research into gifted education demonstrates, unless properly supported with a well-thought-out, differentiated curriculum and other learning aides, gifted children generally do worse in mixed-ability classes compared to separate or accelerated classes.

Why Do Schools Resist Ability Grouping?

If kids and their teachers are struggling in mixed-ability classrooms, why are schools resistant to grouping students by ability?

Ability grouping has become mixed-up with our ideas on and how we have dealt with racism over the years. Consequently, each attempted fix has created an increasingly complicated mess, piling errors on top of errors.

With the introduction of compulsory schooling in America in the 1800s, vocal and powerful people emerged who believed in the separation of children in school based on the "average" ability of the whole group, not on the ability of the individual. People and organizations, such as Francis Galton, considered the founder of gifted research, the faculty of the Carnegie Institute, and the board of the Rockefeller Foundation deeply believed that real ability differences existed between races and socioeconomic classes. Just like today, people eager to sell ideas liked to manipulate scientific findings to dress up their beliefs.

In the 1920s, such people used IQ tests. People liked the idea that IQ was a de facto marker for socioeconomic status. Based on the results of the flawed tests, the wealthy did appear smarter, so separating out the wealthier "smarter" folks from the poorer "less smart" folks seemed like a good idea. The subsequent school system locked children from lower socioeconomic backgrounds out of advanced learning and shunted them early into less rigorous vocational streams. Naturally, this ensured these children did not have the necessary skills to get into higher education. Proponents called this process "tracking."

In first grade, Mirita's parents noticed that she was resisting going to school and would often need sick days. Their family doctor noted that she seemed depressed. When they asked Mirita what was wrong, she said that though she really enjoyed helping other kids, it would be nice to learn something new in school. Though the school was reluctant, after a meeting with her parents, they agreed that the parents could provide supplementary material at school for her to learn. Mirita's parents are hopeful that this will help to bring their little girl back. ~Gifted/2e Survey

Tracking was a stealthy way to segregate, and the deep flaws in the IQ tests of the time catered to many people's prejudices. It took a lot of people an awful lot of time researching and campaigning to expose the wrongs of tracking until it was finally removed. But the removal of tracking from the education system has not fixed the problem in any country with a substantial historically repressed population, whether the United States, Canada, France, United Kingdom, Australia, New Zealand, or elsewhere.

Despite our modern IQ tests being completely different and much fairer (though still problematic), the bad smell of tracking means ability grouping and IQ tests are still deeply frowned upon. Many schools often have no ability grouping at all, poorly funded and ad hoc gifted services, and a tendency to use achievement tests instead of IQ tests if programs are even available. These reactionary approaches still fail gifted children from lower socioeconomic backgrounds, as a lack of government funding means gifted classes often rely on school- or parent-based funding to exist. Consequently, poorer communities continue to miss out. When combined with the ongoing lack of understanding of giftedness, this system leaves gifted minority children just as overlooked and underserved as with tracking.

CHAPTER 4

Giftedness is Complicated

Like most science, gifted research is a moving target. If we look at the history of gifted research, we discover that descriptions of what giftedness is, where it shows up, and what it looks like keep changing. Sometimes an idea, either in research or otherwise, hits the zeitgeist in just the right way and boom— a new myth is created. This happens with old, well-and-truly-debunked, yet persistent ideas and with ideas that initially look true, at least until the science shows otherwise.

As science gets better at describing and recognizing giftedness, the label changes to match. Though not a comprehensive tour of those changes—eighty-plus years cannot be compressed so easily—the following highlights a few of these ideas, particularly those that keep popping up again and again, like flotsam on the beach.

Myth: Early Ripe, Early Rot

The myth of "early ripe, early rot" has been around for a long time—from Keats, dying of consumption; to Mozart, dying of who knows what; to Galois, killed in a duel just prior to the French revolution—everyone believed children who "bloomed early" were destined to burn out young. Not terribly scientific.

Lewis Terman had a bee in his bonnet about this myth, which is why he started his longitudinal study, *Genetic Studies of Genius*, in the 1920s. Terman's study wasn't the only one, with at least half a dozen longitudinal studies being done since. Not surprisingly, gifted children grew into gifted adults, and the vast majority still worked and thought once they left adolescence. They were not doomed to lives of torment or early death.

In fact, from these studies,[29] we now know that gifted people:

- live longer.

- have better long-term physical health.

- have above average educational attainment.

- get to higher levels than average in their professions.

But this myth was given teeth due to the extremely well-publicized life of William Sidis, a mathematical child prodigy in the early 1900s. Considered a public figure from an early age, the press of the time did not treat Sidis kindly, nor endorse his parents' choices for his education. (His father wrote a book on how to "train" a genius.) As the years passed, the press kept following him around, so Sidis became increasingly reclusive. He hated being in the public eye. He even stopped researching mathematics. The press dubbed it burnout due to being pushed in childhood and continued to follow everything he did. Whenever the press showed up, Sidis would go do something else. But he was never really able to escape. No matter what he did (including menial labor), he was always tabloid fodder.

Nearly 100 years later, we're still haunted by the ghost of William Sidis. In the misguided belief that acceleration will do them harm, gifted students are often locked out of whole or part grade acceleration. Yet studies on acceleration or radical acceleration (more than two to three grades acceleration over a child's K-12 education) do not back up this thinking.[30] For exceptionally and profoundly gifted children, acceleration provides positive effects that last a lifetime, including higher academic achievement, better social adjustment, and greater happiness. Acceleration is one of the best and most cost-effective ways to help gifted children. We even have a step-by-step procedure to help schools decide how and when to accelerate, called the Iowa Acceleration Scale from the Belin-Blank Center at the University of Iowa.[31]

Myth: The Gifted Will Always Succeed, Even if Given No Chances

In science, as in life, often we fix one problem only to create another.

By trying to show that gifted people were not going to burn out in early childhood, Lewis Terman accidently created this next myth. His "Termites" were high achieving with excellent life outcomes, and somewhere along the way that became mixed up with the idea that by doing so well, gifted children needed no help at all.

But in many ways, Terman was a better human than a researcher. When he saw his Termites hurting, he would step in and help. He could not bear to see them do badly. Terman effectively became a mentor for many of his subjects.

Unfortunately, Terman also missed data, probably for the same reason: he wanted his Termites to do well. Over the lifetime of the study, his subjects committed suicide at three times the normal rate. Observations from large-scale populations backs up this number. In fact, rates of suicide appear to be quadratic: as a person's IQ goes outside the normal range, either higher or lower, the likelihood of suicide increases.[32] In fact, recent research has found a higher-than-average amount of psychological and neurological diseases and diagnoses in those with IQs in the top two percent.[33] This research seems to contradict other research which found less than average amounts of psychological and neurological diseases and diagnoses; most of those earlier studies had results for only up to the top 10 percent of IQs. Clearly, more work is needed. In the meantime, studies suggest that the incidence of neurological and psychological differences and disabilities might actually be parabolic, not linear. Regardless, evidence suggests that far from being fine on their own, gifted children and adults may struggle without supports, particularly if they have underlying health or neurological differences.

Even the stories we tell about genius appearing from nowhere and needing no supports are, at best, simplifications. Take the story we tell about Einstein: he wrote his papers on special relativity and light while working as a patent clerk, cut off from the academic world. The real story is far more interesting.

When Einstein was working as a patent clerk, he was in regular correspondence with many scientists, including his friends, the Curies. His wife at the time, Mileva Einstein (née Marić), was also a physicist who attended the same university and worked alongside him during their undergraduate work. She even shared the same topic with him for their dissertation diplomas (quite an unusual achievement for a woman in the early twentieth-century). Though hotly debated, whether Mileva Einstein contributed to her husband's work after this point is a question that will probably never be answered. What we can say is that Einstein was certainly not isolated from people who understood his work.

We are often questioned on whether we are "pushing" our daughter. I have had many friends question me, worried that my girl will burn out, or be so socially maladjusted that she'll never have any friends. They've even said it's unfair that she will miss out on the prom or won't be able to drive or drink at university. I don't really know how to handle those conversations—my girl is pulling me along, not the other way around! I figure we'll deal with them when they come up, but for now I'm focused on keeping her happy rather than worrying about some hypothetical future. ~Gifted/2e Survey

When we look at many other famous "lone geniuses," a similar story emerges: their life has been rewritten, airbrushing out friends, colleges, and spouses who worked alongside or offered intellectual support. A prime example is Ada Lovelace's support and contribution to Charles Babbage's ideas on a universal machine, also known as the computer. Lovelace recognized that Babbage's machine had applications beyond pure calculation. She consequently published the first algorithm to be used by such a machine. Though the degree of her contributions remains disputed by some, many historians and biographers regard her as the first computer programmer.

The lone genius is a compelling story, but it's rarely true.

Myth: All Nobel Laureates Are Gifted

Our culture has a perverse desire to rewrite the history of successful people to show how they were destined for greatness. In fact, this very idea kicked off the first work on giftedness, Francis Galton's book, *Hereditary Genius.* We like to look through an icon's history and show how their mind or actions in childhood naturally led to success.

Often, successful people, particularly people like Nobel Laureates, are labeled as gifted after the fact. Lewis Terman's coresearcher, Catherine Cox, did just that when she published a retrospective attempt to estimate the IQ of famous people from the past. Early researchers loved the idea that every person who did amazing things must have been a "superhero in waiting."[34] Interestingly, Lewis Terman accidently managed to prove this false. When he started his longitudinal study of gifted children in the 1920s, he found his subjects through testing large populations of children in schools. While these children statistically grew up to have higher-than-average salaries and jobs, none of them won any Nobel Prizes or Fields Medals. Considering Terman's sample size was small compared to the population of the entire planet, perhaps this is not really a surprise. Interestingly, one of the students tested and *not* accepted into Terman's studies was William Shockley, a white, middle-class boy who should have been the perfect candidate. But young William tested as neurotypical.

In 1970, William Shockley won the Nobel Prize for the invention of the transistor.

Gifted History 101

To understand a little about the complicated history of gifted research, it's useful to highlight a few of the milestones along the way that reformed our ideas about intelligence, and how to measure it. This understanding will also make clearer what a school means when its brochure proclaims it follows Gagne's model of giftedness, or a teacher union proclaims it believes in multiple intelligences, or what exactly is going on with Renzulli and his three rings.

1926: Leta Defines Gifted

One of the icons of modern gifted research, Leta Hollingworth, was the first researcher to study the behaviors and challenges gifted children faced. Her most important work, *Gifted Children* (1926), was also the first to use the word.

Leta was interested in helping the children with their unique problems and focused on discovering the best learning environment for gifted children. Her longitudinal study in 1942 was also the first on profoundly gifted children. (A longitudinal study involves repeated observation of variables, in this case, people, over long periods of time.) Being a rare female researcher at that time, she understood that giftedness was not limited to just men, or any demographic, and insisted children from all backgrounds, particularly minorities, be accepted when she opened the Speyer School in New York. The Speyer School focused on social-emotional learning and social coaching—programs which bear striking similarities to programs now used for children on the autism spectrum.

1970s: Renzulli and His Rings

In the 1970s, researchers finally began to look at how environment and opportunity affected scores on IQ or achievement tests. Dr. Joseph Renzulli, Professor of Educational Psychology at the University of Connecticut, was one of the first to note that high ability was a mix between nature and nurture. He called it a "three-ring conception of giftedness," and believed that for a child to demonstrate giftedness, he or she would require above average ability, creativity, and task commitment. Renzulli's research was one of the first to acknowledge that gifted children did not automatically succeed.

1980s: The Wishful Thinking of Multiple Intelligences

The "Theory of Multiple Intelligences" was created in the 1980s by Dr. Howard Gardner, Professor of the Harvard Graduate School of Education at Harvard University, in an attempt to create a more egalitarian ideal of giftedness. He believed many types of giftedness were not covered by IQ testing and suggested eight new categories: musical-rhythmic, visual-spatial, verbal-linguistic, logical-mathematical, bodily-kinesthetic, interpersonal, intrapersonal, and naturalistic. This appealed to teachers and other educators, as they could then expand the definition of giftedness. But Gardner's categories lacked scientific rigor, with the categories being either untestable or just another aspect of general IQ (which defeated the purpose of new categories of giftedness). Gardner's ideas were eventually debunked in gifted research, but nevertheless hung on in the wider community. Unfortunately, it's created ongoing problems by making giftedness seem subjective.

1990s: Gagné Gets Rid of Equating Achievement with Gifted

In the 1990s, Professor Robert Gagné, with his "Differentiated Model of Giftedness and Talent," was able to show a difference between potential and performance, in other words, between having ability and displaying it. Though his model basically created the category of gifted underachievers, finding these children remained a challenge.

Eliminating Bias: An Ongoing Quest

The research on eliminating biases in IQ tests has been, in many ways, a belated application of the Hippocratic Oath, *primum non nocere* (first, do no harm), as researchers have tried to figure out how to stop IQ tests being misused and abused, and reconsidered where gifted people are found.

As previously discussed, cultural biases in IQ tests are not new. Though the difference in scores between cultures was first noticed in the 1920s, the problem was not addressed until the 1940s, with the seminal work of Dr. Martin Jenkins. Dr. Raymond Cattel, one of the founders of modern empirical psychology, later created his "culture fair" tests, in part as a reaction to how IQ tests had been used by eugenicists. (As the horrors of the Nazis became known, eugenics had finally fallen out of favor.)

The 1970s brought further changes, when the test was expanded using the System of Multicultural Pluralistic Assessment instrument, influenced by ideas from the civil rights movement which forced researchers to look at how their tests had been used to justify segregation. When new biases due to language were found in the 1990s, researchers created the Universal Nonverbal Intelligence Test on which the now widely used Raven's Matrices is based.

Work on these problems is still ongoing, with pioneering work continuing with researchers creating a Bill of Rights for Gifted Students of Color.[35]

Yet despite decades of improvements, when the questions on IQ tests become more complex, the score gap still increases for minorities. We now know that this is not due to the tasks being more challenging, but because the questions require more culture-specific know-how. Test writers tend to come from the white middle class and unwittingly allow their cultural biases to seep into the test. This makes it harder for kids outside that culture bubble to get high scores, regardless of whether they take verbal or nonverbal IQ tests. When cultural groups are sorted based on education and income, a lot of the difference vanishes. But not all.

Even with all the work that has been done, our ideas about IQ remain very "Western." The less Western a culture, the harder Western-trained researchers find it to figure out what to test. We know that different cultures value and display intelligence differently, and our brains are very plastic (see chapter 6). This creates problems when we use the wrong tests to find gifted children.

The Flaws with Almost All Gifted Research

When we look at the literature on giftedness, the sheer number of different definitions is astounding!

Though partly attributable to changing ideas on intelligence, these differences more often than not have their roots in convenience, expediency, and lack of money. Testing children on what they know and have accomplished (standardized tests) is easier and cheaper than testing them on how they think (IQ and other cognitive and behavioral tests). Much of the education literature assumes these two things are interchangeable but, when looked at more closely, this only holds true for children from stable middle-class backgrounds, not the wider community.

Most educational research uses high scores on knowledge-based tests as a proxy for giftedness. This happens either directly when researchers use their own standards-based tests or indirectly when their study picks students only from gifted classes or pull-out programs which, for cost reasons, use high classroom scores for entry. Whether they mean to or not, these researchers miss gifted students who are struggling, failing, and/or low-income, or who do not fit the gifted stereotype. As a result, most research in education (rather than psychology or medicine) on giftedness concludes that gifted kids, on average, do better than neurotypical children. Not surprising that when you only select kids who succeed, you come to the radical conclusion that, well, they all succeed.

Understandably, all of this tells us little about gifted kids who are not high achieving, or even how many there are.

An IQ test takes time. It requires real expertise to administer and interpret the results. When IQ tests are used to select children, researchers know these kids are definitely gifted. But though these researchers go to the enormous expense of testing their subjects, their studies remain unintentionally flawed.

Consider that due to the expense of IQ testing and difficulty finding large amounts of gifted children, most research focuses on children who come to research or medical centers. Whether they mean to or not, these centers are prefiltering their subjects based on the wealth and/or education of their parents, as they have enough time and money to keep pushing for answers. Additionally, the researchers test more children with behaviors potentially caused by disabilities, as those get a referral. In fact, most of this testing only receives funding if there are unusual behaviors or a suspicion of disabilities, which understandably skews the profile of what giftedness looks like.

So, which is it? Does giftedness equal success, or does giftedness equal unusual behavior?

We simply do not know.

Unfortunately, very few places have the time, money, and expertise to do the large-scale, culture-blind, longitudinal studies needed to answer this question. Even research that on the surface appears good and works hard to try to reach gifted children who could be missed can accidently prefilter. A good example is the John Hopkins University's Longitudinal Study of Mathematically Precocious Youth, one of the few long-term studies to look at life outcomes for gifted children.[36] This study selects children on the basis of SAT scores administered between the ages of 12 and 13. The SAT is rarely given to children at age 12 or 13, and the fact that the test was administered means that someone—whether a parent, teacher, or other adult mentor—organized the testing. As sitting for the SAT also generally requires a fee, but fee waivers are not given to students who are officially enrolled in ninth grade or lower, low income students without financial support and/or supportive home and school environments are missed.

Children from families who are unaware of gifted characteristics, who do not know about the tests they can request, who might struggle due to language barriers, poverty, or institutional bias are missed in almost all current research on giftedness. This holds true for nearly all the results on gifted characteristics and gifted education. While we do not have cheap and easy solutions, we must find a way to study these children. We need to know what gifted children look like when they're not wealthy and well-educated and when they don't have mentors and accommodations, because that is the reality for many gifted children. And at present, we don't know much about them at all.

CHAPTER 5

What is Twice-Exceptional?

Understanding your child's differences can be a long process, requiring an awful lot of testing, nail biting, and fuzzy maybes from concerned doctors. Brains are complicated things to begin with, so when you deal with brains very different from average, they become even more complicated. Couple a gifted brain with the neurological or physical differences of a disability, and we go way off the map.

We call this level of difference—gifted with an additional neurological or physical disability—twice exceptional (2e), or gifted learning disabled (GLD). Currently, we believe that about 14 percent of gifted children have a co-occurring disability,[37] though this percentage varies depending on the medical definitions in different countries.

According to recent work by Dr. Karen Rogers, twice-exceptional children, particularly those with communication or physical challenges, do not test well on IQ tests.[38] Twice-exceptional children will normally test in the top 16 percent on an IQ test, but often have at least one subscale score in the top two percent. Often, no score can be calculated at all.

This happened with my daughter, who hit the floor in some subtests and the ceiling in others. My daughter, a master at not answering questions, pulled faces in the testing center's two-way mirror and hid under the table. The best our psychologist, an expert in 2e issues, could do was estimate her IQ.

Regardless of the specific percentage, whether a child's disability or giftedness is picked up depends on myriad factors. For some kids, their set of disabling behaviors is so large that their extraordinary ability is glossed over, ignored, or never found. Consequently, they often do not have the opportunity to show what they can do. Antonio, a highly gifted child on the autism spectrum with a mild form of muscular dystrophy that affects his extremities, exemplifies this disconnect. When Antonio was young, his parents did not realize he was gifted. In fact, they thought he was mentally impaired: he did not walk until he was three and a half, nor speak until he was four. Instead, Antonio would sit and scream for hours. But once he was able to speak and interact, things changed. He was tested using the Wechsler Intelligence Scale for Children (WISC) with an estimated IQ in the 160-170 range. Finding the balance between his competing needs has had a profound impact on his family in how they interact with Antonio, including their expectations, day-to-day routines, and nonroutine events like holidays and vacations.

But for many children, the opposite happens: their abilities are so extraordinary that their deficits are either overlooked, or they somewhat compensate using their amazing problem-solving abilities to come up with ways of achieving on their own. Consider the gifted dyslexic child who uses her eidetic memory to memorize words based on the first and last letters as well as the number of letters to be able to "read" fluently; or the gifted autistic adult who spends an enormous amount of time studying the way other people move, teaching himself to mimic this so completely that no one can tell he has any problems at all, despite his internal mass of confusion and misunderstanding. Even for those closest—parents, siblings, partners—seeing the disability underneath the ability can be hard.

For the twice-exceptional child, masking can be a way of life, and even they might not know exactly how different they are. This often happens for twice-exceptional girls, particularly with "invisible" disabilities like ADHD. A lot of research has focused on the misdiagnosis of gifted children as ADHD when their abundant energy is mismanaged in the classroom (which leads to the diagnosis rather than the needed acceleration), but children with inattentive ADHD, particularly girls, are often overlooked. These girls tend to be quiet, as the hyperactivity plays out in their heads. Because they're never challenged intellectually in the classroom, their severe executive function problems remain unnoticed. A child who always instantly knows the answer does not raise any red flags, so no one catches on that she has no ability to plan how to learn or put together a project. In fact, gifted ADHD girls might not notice any problems until they suddenly have cope with life outside school, when they have to balance finances or plan study schedules for complicated university subjects. Instead, they muddle through without a diagnosis, which holds true for quite a number of twice-exceptional children, with a range of disabilities, including autism, schizophrenia, Sensory Processing Disorder (SPD), and numerous others.

The same masking that occurs for neural issues also can happen for physical disabilities. For example, dyspraxia—a disability involving a lack of muscle control due to brain wiring—is difficult to diagnose in gifted children. Sometimes, their accelerated gifted development offsets their delay in gross and fine motor skills. They look developmentally normal, until suddenly they do not. The effort to compensate for having a hard-to-control body means that 2e kids can get tired very quickly. This exhaustion leads twice-exceptional kids to struggle to physically or mentally carry out tasks, even when they understand what to do.

Communication difficulties due to hearing and/or auditory processing issues also play a part in 2e issues. Twice-exceptional children with mild to moderate levels of hearing or vision loss or auditory processing problems can compensate so thoroughly that they're not identified for either of their exceptionalities. A child with fine motor control and creative drive can mask the fact that her vision is poor.

This happened with my daughter. Her extraordinary visual-spatial abilities compensated for her near legal blindness. Despite seeing the world as a wobbly distorted blur, she loved to paint and draw and was able to write the alphabet. Even though her father and I have execrable vision, so vision problems were on our radar, our daughter's ability to compensate delayed our seeking answers. Once we did, she ended up with the answers and support she needs (purple glasses, which she loves, and vision therapy, which she does not).

Myth: Gifted Kids Cannot Have Disabilities

The myth that gifted kids cannot have disabilities plays a large role in the misidentification of gifted and 2e kids. Knowing how often 2e children mask their disabilities and/or abilities in the home environment, it makes sense that these different types of masking also happen in the classroom, which contributes to the difficulty in identifying twice-exceptional kids within school. As a result, most gifted programs do not acknowledge or cater to the challenges faced by twice-exceptional children. Programs which identify giftedness based on criteria not adapted for kids with special needs, such as focusing on unaided performance measures or all-round achievement testing, will consequently overlook twice-exceptional kids.

Twice-exceptional children often are misdiagnosed or go undiagnosed due to:

- Their scores on standard or psychological tests being average, which masks large differences

- Comparisons to children their own age, rather than to their expected ability based on their level of giftedness

- Their lower scores not falling far below the normal range

- Their compensation for their problems, which means their lower scores will not be as low in comparison to their deficits

- Not considering the large differences between their strengths and weaknesses

Even if a 2e child receives a diagnosis, she may not qualify for services. The design of many disability services will disqualify a high IQ child from receiving help. For example, the provision for support services in the school, whether provided in the classroom or for external tests and exams, may completely separate services for gifted students from ones for disabled students, even when a child can qualify for both. This can, for example, affect the physical supports for dyspraxic gifted children or learning supports for dyslexic gifted children. In order to receive needed services for even obvious physical disabilities, many families are forced to remove all references to giftedness—or vice versa.

For these children, the myth gets in the way, and the often hidden nature of twice-exceptionality makes the myth hard to refute. Research that looked at the attitudes of special needs teachers in preservice found that even when the evidence indicated it, special needs children were much less likely to be referred for gifted testing or gifted services.[39]

Acknowledging that a child with extraordinary abilities might also have extraordinary struggles, or vice versa, can prove difficult for those tasked with providing services for students in need. This goes double when families, friends, teachers, administrators, and society in general see disability as somehow "less than," rather than as a difference requiring support.

CHAPTER 6

Taking Another Look at Neurology

Every now and again, my husband and I have what we call a "So, how do you think?" talk. We start with a simple question, one that seems basic, even obvious. Something that would never normally get questioned. Our most recent was, "So, how do you see?" My husband sees everything as patterns. He does not see a chair as a "chair" but instead as a shape. A bed is not a "bed" but a shape, and so on. Occasionally, he also "sees" sound (i.e., synesthesia). For him, high-pitched loud noises are "seen" as light so bright it hurts. My way of seeing differs to my husband's and, I suspect, many other people. I call it "jumping focus." My vision constantly cycles, spending a fraction of a second on each brightly colored object in a room before jumping to the next in a never-ending cycle. That's how my ADHD brain passes the time of day.

Sometimes simple questions lead to complicated, fascinating answers.

One simple question is, why does IQ vary so much between different groups and across cultures?

For a start, poverty and a lack of resources have a huge impact. As the level of poverty goes up, the average IQ goes down. But this only holds true for the very worst levels of poverty like starvation, long-term homelessness, and a lack of access to basic healthcare. But if lack of money doesn't limit a child's access to opportunities such as extension programs, poor, gifted kids with lower IQ scores do just as well as wealthy gifted kids when given challenging work. As their IQ tests don't reflect this, something is obviously wrong but what?

Researchers have spent a lot of time and money trying to answer just that question. They have rewritten tests after identifying the cultural biases. But despite their best efforts, they haven't isolated exactly where the problem lies.

It turns out the problem might not be with the IQ tests at all. Instead, the answer might just lie in the neurology of the brain.

Human brains are incredibly plastic, as seen in the eternal tug-of-war in the nature-versus-nurture debate. Environment plays a huge role in how our brains develop. For years, brain researchers thought that only the worst environmental conditions, such as lack of access to food, would cause the brain to develop differently. But they were wrong. Through epigenetics, we now know that our environment can alter the chemical pathways in our brains and even our DNA.

Mucking Up Neurology: It's All Plastic Fantastic

To understand how environment relates to the average population differences in IQ tests, we need to take a side trip into basic economics, and the Kalahari Desert.

A key concept in economics deals with models of risk and how people handle it. Noted mathematician John Nash called this Game Theory, and economists subsequently assumed that there were certain fundamental "panhuman" ways of thinking. In 2000, Joseph Henrich, an evolutionary biologist, checked that idea by going out and testing whether people really all thought the same way.

It turns out that they do not.

Henrich's results have since been replicated around the world. Different groups have fundamentally different ways of playing the "Ultimatum Game," a simple game where two people share a sum of money. Some cultures emphasized getting the most amount of money (the original assumption), while others emphasized giving away the most amount of money. Clearly, culture is more plastic than the theories allowed, which has since lead to the reexamination of many fundamental economic assumptions.

Meanwhile, the San people in the Kalahari(and the Yukatek Maya in Mexico, and Native Americans in Wisconsin…and in many other rural communities), have overturned another assumption: the Müller-Lyer illusion[40].

You may have seen this optical illusion at some point:

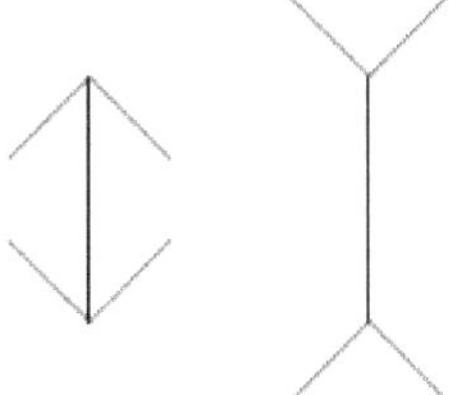

The line with the arrows pointing inward looks longer, but both lines are actually the same length. This optical illusion fools most people in developed cultures, but not members of traditional hunter-gatherer societies, who see both lines as exactly the same length. Why?

By not growing up in a built environment, surrounded by buildings, they don't learn to interpret straight lines as three-dimensional shapes. Until these people were tested, researchers assumed the Müller-Lyer illusion was hardwired into our brains. Even though babies in developed cultures can do this, it's actually a plastic ability which develops early in the right environment.

Just like the assumption about the Müller-Lyer illusion, the assumptions in the models of how brains work muck up any testing. Without testing a wide range of people, results from culture or environment will be mistaken for universal abilities.

The University Student: A Universal Human?

When university researchers need people for a study, they jump over a number of hurdles: ethics committees, population sizes, and so on. Getting enough people to act as guinea pigs for their experiments is challenging. Luckily for researchers, a ready population is at hand: university students and employees! Unfortunately, as most brain research is done in Western countries, this population is mostly White or Asian. University students are also usually economically middle- and upper-class, as fewer kids from working class backgrounds tend to go on to higher education. These groups even have a label, WEIRD: Western, Educated, Industrialized, Rich and Democratic. Almost all research has been done on young people with this profile. For psychology, a staggering 96 percent of all research is done on WEIRD kids, and it's not much better in other branches of biomedical research.[41]

Researchers assumed this was OK for research into how our brains work, because they believed that mild poverty and/or cultural differences did not have a fine-grain effect on brain development. It was an easy assumption—and an economical one. Testing diverse populations can be expensive, especially on tight research budgets.

As a result, we have a very good idea of how wealthy university students' brains work, particularly if they're American, but are a little hazy about the rest. If we don't know how university students' brains differ from everyone else's brains, we can't watch out for those differences in IQ tests.

The fundamental assumptions on what is hardwired and what is plastic in the brain are out of whack. All this goes a long way to describing the current problems with IQ tests.

Researchers are now finally looking at how culture and environment affect the brain and behavior differences across cultures and environments. These include tests on object recognition, geometric frames of reference, motive attribution, and many more. We still have a way to go, but research looks like it's finally heading in the right direction

CHAPTER 7

Where to From Here?

So where do we go from here? How do we reconcile all the myths and baggage? How do we not fall victim to the myths of gifted past and find the educational options that will work for all types of gifted kids?

Understanding the myths around giftedness and the limits of our current system provides us the opportunity to address both issues. When people are trapped within the framework created by these myths, programs and opportunities for gifted children can look difficult, unfair, and expensive. But by proactively addressing the underlying fears of these myths, finding common ground, fighting the inertia of a system, and creating a new way of looking at education, gifted families can rewrite these assumptions. This will create the opportunity for all gifted children to get an education that works for them.

Myth: Giftedness is Easily Accommodated in a Regular Classroom

A persistent myth lurking around educational establishments suggests that teachers can easily differentiate for the learning needs of gifted students, and they can do this without extra help or training of any kind. Though the research literature into gifted education backs up none of this, the myth persists for three reasons:

1. Money: Training teachers and hiring aides can be costly.

2. Time: Designing a proper differentiated curriculum appropriate for different ability levels takes time, classroom and materials development support, and commitment to organize and support whole or part accelerations.

3. Ignorance: "More of the same" or "slightly faster that regular speed" are incorrectly assumed to be the same as true differentiation.

As previously discussed, gifted children brains develop at different rates and in different ways, potentially leading to deep asynchrony (when a child's ability in one area is vastly different to his level in another). Even without twice-exceptionality, asynchronous development creates a real problem for differentiating in the classroom because of the way lessons are designed.

For instance, math learning may be delayed due to handwriting difficulties or accelerated reading or writing learning held back due to a delayed ability in math or science. Because lessons are designed around the concept of a typical learner, gifted children can be locked out of learning more advanced material and feel shame at not being equally capable in their weaker fields. But universal giftedness is the exception. Asynchrony is the actual norm.

Carefully considered subject acceleration often produces a better, cost-effective, and less wasteful solution for many gifted children compared to differentiating in an age-based classroom.

Gifted children can also learn material in different ways. Highly to profoundly gifted children often find it easier to learn in chunks—from the most abstract idea back to the more specific examples (also called "whole-to-part" learning). Since this method is the reverse of the typical curriculum, teachers would find it difficult to implement in a mixed-ability classroom, which probably explains why many families with highly to profoundly gifted[39] children end up homeschooling or part-time schooling.

Outside of academics, gifted children may need support in learning how their thinking differs from other children. They often expect their age-mates to want the same type of play and friendship as they do. If teachers were trained to understand how mental and physical age differences can cause problems, this would provide a more positive social experience for gifted children and other children with differences from the norm.

Gifted children can also be extremely sensitive and have outsized emotional responses to situations,[42] and may experience clinically significant, crippling levels of perfectionism. Learning ways to handle their outsized emotions and mental vulnerabilities is vital to a healthy educational environment for gifted children and may be almost as important as subject acceleration.

Jacob is profoundly gifted, twice-exceptional, and is technically in grade three. His school has substantially adapted his learning environment—he writes using an iPad or a laptop which helps with his dyspraxia; he presents his learning at once as a whole idea, using a delivery method of his choice (e.g., fiction story, Power Point presentation), rather than using quizzes; all his tasks are broken down into small steps and written down in lists; he has a differentiated math program; and the school organized with the local university to bring in a tutor for his advanced areas—physics and computing. Jacob enjoys being in a mixed-age class because he can be challenged academically with the older kids, but also has kids there his own age.[43]

Fighting Inertia

Our culture simultaneously idolizes and denigrates gifted minds. With no "right" answer, but plenty of misinformation, often dressed up with a veneer of bureaucratic respectability, navigating this dichotomy proves challenging for gifted children and their families.

Inevitably, this has led to a culture clash between the reality of the gifted person's experience and the cultural trappings with which giftedness has been burdened.

Idolizing and denigrating do not mesh. Whether dealing with envy at perceived advantages or coping with misunderstandings from mis-aligned expectations of their growth and development, gifted children and their families struggle for understanding, acceptance, and support.

Problems? Getting appropriate services at school. I have learned that sometimes I know more than my child's teachers, and I can't be afraid to speak up. ~Gifted/2e Survey

Our biggest challenge is finding families and supports—it can be very lonely being the gifted parent of a gifted child in a small rural school in a rural province. ~Gifted/2e Survey

Helping her feel comfortable in her own skin. Even if she has all of the "right" clothes, etc., she's still quirky (and adorable!). [...] She qualified for the Summer Experience at Duke Tip. Very exciting! Not so exciting? Telling her we cannot afford the $4,000 to send her. ~Gifted/2e Survey

The thing is, it doesn't have to be this way. Many of the problems faced by gifted families mirror the challenges faced by families with disabilities. And they also often are met with the same response: somehow the child must adapt to the environment without the support they need to thrive.

Different children and children who don't fit will always be a problem if we keep to a system that expects all children to learn, think, and move in the same ways. And it doesn't matter what that difference is: moving to the beat of your own drum is hard when you're expected to be in the marching band and play the exact same tune.

But it doesn't have be hard. And there are already solutions out there just waiting to be picked up.

Outside-the-Box Education

Struggling against a system can seem impossible. But an increasing number of people are seeking solutions, whether as individuals, in groups, in traditional schools, or in alternative education. These are often not difficult or expensive to do and include many different solutions to the same issues.

Mastery-Based School Progression

Many primary schools in Australia have thrown out age-based learning. By scheduling subjects at the same time across the whole school (e.g., math in the morning, English after lunch), the school makes it easy and natural for students to move between classes based on their ability level.

Children can test out of their current level and move up to the next grouping. Each teacher has only a small handful of students in each group, with a limited number of groups per class. Though the teachers end up with the same number of students overall, they do not have to differentiate over such a wide ability range, which makes their jobs easier.

Rather than grading children using a traditional A through F measurement, children follow a mastery-type program. Remedial work fits easily into this framework, as does extension, which removes the stigma for being either behind or ahead. This innovative way of organizing does not take more money or require more specialists than the traditional model, yet it manages to help students at all ability levels.

Giving Children Control

Templestowe High in Melbourne, Australia, has embraced the idea that children should be in charge of their own learning. While still using a standard classroom structure, this public school lets children advocate for their own subject acceleration and outside classroom opportunities, such as apprenticeships. Willing to adapt to students' needs, when administrators found that external goals, such as getting a high score, were impeding student learning, the school decided to move away from forcing students to do high-stress year 12 exams.[44]

Child-centered learning is well-established in the US through the Sudbury democratic school-system. Professor Peter Grey from Boston College has done extensive research on Sudbury schools and the importance of play-based learning. On average, children in these systems do as well as or better than children in more traditional school models. They also tend to have a higher number of graduates pursuing creative or entrepreneurial careers.[45]

Umbrella Schools

Beach High School, based in California, is probably one of the longer-running examples of an umbrella school. It allows children an alternative graduation pathway by helping them put together a portfolio. This portfolio demonstrates how their personal learning path has allowed them to cover all the material they need for graduation.[46]

Part-Time Schooling

In many countries, part-time schooling has become a path to meeting the diverse needs of gifted and twice-exceptional students. Some schools allow homeschool students to enroll in courses specifically set up for part-time homeschoolers, while some countries and states allow any child to enroll as a part-time student. For twice-exceptional students, part-time attendance offers a way for them to balance their desire for group learning in a school environment with their own one-on-one learning needs being met at home.

Cloud-Based Learning

Dr. Sugata Mitra, from Newcastle University in England, is a pioneer in child-centered remote learning. His groundbreaking work set out to test assumptions on what is needed for optimal learning. These experiments showed how little was necessary:

- Open-ended access to resources, particularly the internet

- A safe environment to explore learning

- Small groups and child-led learning

- An adult mentor to empathetically listen when children describe their learning

Dr. Mitra has turned his attention more recently to creating a "School in the Cloud," with easily put-together learning environments that foster creative group learning. He even has what he calls a "Granny Cloud," where a dynamic list of retirees can be accessed on Skype so students from around the world can connect to them and chat.[47]

Micro-Schools

An educational option which combines the best of the many alternative approaches is micro-schools. Families banding together, innovative teachers tired of the status quo, and administrators wanting to create a better learning environment have all started micro-schools in their communities. These schools cater to specific educational and social needs for niche students. Micro-schools may offer full- or part-time enrollment, sometimes both. In her book, *Micro-Schools: Creating Personalized Learning on a Budget,* progressive educator and micro-school founder Jade Rivera discusses why "micro-schools for gifted and twice-exceptional children are well designed to meet the needs of these outlier students."[48]

Resource Rooms and Sheds

Another growing phenomenon is places filled with learning resources where students can drop in at any time. From Men's Sheds, which foster the passing down of crafting skills between generations, to learning labs for children with autism, which have a strong tech focus on the practicalities of electronics and computing, these spaces are designed with exploration, knowledge sharing, and creative thinking in mind.[49]

Finding Common Ground

 The old myths make it easy to build a narrative of fear: fear of the "other" and a fear of somehow being less than others. This fear narrative has been used by segregationists and eugenicists over the years to bolster their own ideas and fed into a simplistic story with little basis in reality. Conversely, people who stand against these ideas have used that same fear to funnel their dislike toward easy targets: families and children who, from the outside, seem to embody all the things that the myths claim as true. Acknowledging this fear is a very important first step to unpacking all these gifted myths.

But we can't just ignore this history, either. Fighting for services for gifted kids does not mean those families oppose or want to reduce services for the disabled or kids from marginalized backgrounds. In many ways, the services that these groups need have more in common with gifted needs than is obvious from the outside.

Leta Hollingworth's holistic services for profoundly gifted kids included social-emotional education and explicit instruction in understanding people who think differently as a neurological minority, which exemplified this crossover of services. These same ideas form a core part of best-practice interventions for children on the autism spectrum.

Additionally, a large portion of gifted children experience sensory processing differences. Estimates suggest that over one-third of highly-gifted children have Sensory Processing Disorder (SPD).[42] Given that SPD is also extremely common for children with ADHD, autism, and Obsessive-Compulsive Disorder (OCD), being aware of the sensory challenges is one of the many potential places for a common ground between the gifted and special needs communities. For example, accommodations and services for sensory regulation or having classrooms assessed by occupational therapists and set up in sensory-friendly ways could enhance the lives of children in both of these communities.

When we:

- start to decouple achievement from giftedness;

The first few years of family life were extremely stressful wondering why his behavior was so challenging and why he was different to all the other kids around us. Everyone gave us negative labels, and we were a very stressed family. After his diagnoses, it turned our life around to become a positive, though still challenging, journey of discovery and learning. We have embraced all of his qualities and work with him on the emotional and social stuff every day. We think we have "found ourselves" as a family now, so are more relaxed about being different. ~Gifted/2e Survey

- understand that there is no inevitable stairway to stardom for gifted children;

- understand that achievement is not a natural consequence of ability;

- realize that the opportunities and supports available to each child have a massive impact;

- understand that each child has different – often really different – needs, and supports won't organically just emerge from the ether

...we can start to reorganize how we think about learning and education. When we can naturally accommodate the extreme outliers in a system, rather than shutting them out or denying their existence, then we will be on our way to creating the safe, nurturing environment all our children deserve.

Gifted families, burdened with the myths of having lots of advantages and few disadvantages, and special needs families, burdened with myths of having lots of disadvantages and few advantages, actually share more similarities than differences. As with much in life, the perception of these advantages versus disadvantages—such as sensory sensitivity—depend on the lens through which they're viewed.

By being compassionate and reflecting on the history of giftedness, we can understand that advocating for gifted services which aren't offered equally to minorities or twice-exceptional children undermine the whole idea – indeed the point – of helping gifted children. We have to understand that gifted comes with a lot of cultural baggage. But if families and educators champion programs to help gifted kids from disadvantaged communities, we can start to undo a lot of the muddle and the myths. When gifted programs have the same proportion of minorities and disabled children as the general population, these myths will start to fade.

But it's hard to get people to listen. Who wants to be told that their 'good' actions are doing harm? Even if it's accidental?

We have all, in a way, been held hostage by old, outdated, and fundamentally wrong ideas. And we've been doing the wrong thing for all the right reasons. Because myths offer simple, easy-to-understand stories,

> That myth that gifted kids are advanced in everything? This has been frustrating with my husband's family. She was late tying shoes, etc. Also, that belief that all gifted kids are outgoing, confident leaders who need no support. Why would they have to struggle with anything? ~Gifted/2e Survey

they have a habit of hanging around well beyond their use-by date. Reality is far messier and not easy to compress into simple narratives.

But all is not lost. We need to step beyond these old ideas and find ways to help people understand that gifted people are not a threat, neither godlike nor demons, neither fictional nor superhuman. Gifted people are fundamentally just people. Their brains may work differently—particularly in the case of twice-exceptional kids—but these differences in behavior, ability, and weakness are linked to their genes and brain wiring, not anything threatening. For too long, the idea of helping gifted kids has been seen as something that will hurt others. But it doesn't have to be that way at all. With a bit of imagination, a touch of daring, and a willingness to make education work for everyone, there is a chance to help every child—even the gifted ones.

People may be tempted to say that dealing with this is too difficult, to proclaim that these differences either don't exist or are merely a consequence of different upbringing and opportunity. Yet this is neither a solution nor fair.

When we look at what science has found out about gifted behaviors, gifted brains, and gifted development, and the universal distribution of giftedness across cultural, racial, and socioeconomic boundaries, we must rise up to unshackle ourselves from these myths.

We now have the capacity to look with unbiased eyes and see that different does not mean better or worse. It's just different. And in supporting that difference, we can answer to our better angels, rather than keep on giving credence to the twisted fables from our past.

Recommended Resources
Gifted/2e Issues

2e Newsletter, http://www.2enewsletter.com/

Exceptionally Gifted Children by Miraca U.M. Gross (Routledge 2004)

GHF Learners, http://www.ghflearners.org/

Hoagies Gifted Education Page, http://www.hoagiesgifted.org/

A Nation Deceived: How Schools Hold Back America's Brightest Students by Nicholas Colangelo, Susan G. Assouline, et al. (University of Iowa, 2004)

A Nation Empowered: Evidence Trumps the Excuses Holding Back America's Brightest Students by Susan G. Assouline, Nicholas Colangelo, et al. (University of Iowa, 2015)

The Out-of-Sync Child: Recognizing and Coping with Sensory Processing Disorder by Carol Kranowitz (TarcherPerigee, 2006)

Recommended Resources
Alternate Education

Forging Paths: Beyond Traditional Schooling by Wes Beach (GHF Press, 2012)

"Freedom to Learn" by Peter Grey, https://www.psychologytoday.com/blog/freedom-learn

How Children Learn by John Holt (Da Capo Lifelong Books, 1995)

The Lab, http://thelab.org.au/

Learning in the 21st Century: How to Connect, Collaborate, and Create by Ben Curran and Neil Wetherbee (GHF Press, 2013)

Micro-Schools: Creating Personalized Learning on a Budget by Jade Rivera (GHF Press, 2016)

Acknowledgments

It has been a long journey to get this into print. I have had so many people help me and encourage me to keep going.

To my previous editor, Sarah Wilson, and my current editor Nikki Hegstrom, I wish to give a big thank you. You have both helped get this book over the line.

I would like to thank Corin Barsily Goodwin for encouraging me to write this book in the first place and to Barry Gelston and Celi Toce Trepanier for encouraging me to keep going when the going got tough. Without you folks, this book would not be here.

I would like to thank Pamela Price and the whole Grew Crew for keeping me sane, as well as for your wonderful questions, suggestions, and advice. I also want to send a big thank you to all my friends and family who have put up with my cryptic grumbles – it's been a few years and tears, and you have been fantastic.

I would also specifically like to thank my mum, Mary, and my good friend Lindsay Bignell for wading through my drafts and giving excellent suggestions, as well as listening to my random diatribes on various topics. I could not have done it without you.

And lastly, to my wonderful kids and husband, Tim, who have patiently put up with a very distracted mum and partner over this long journey. They have had to listen to my random rants on this stuff for years, and were so absolutely patient, particularly when I was distracted and everything went cray cray. Tim, bless him, followed Robert Heinlein's advice and discovered wells of calm and patience—and occasionally pushed food into my workspace with a long stick.

This book was written on the lands of the Wurundjeri people of the Kulin Nations and I pay my respect to Elders, past, present and emerging.

Endnotes

1. Mark Leikin, Ilana Waisman and Roza Leikin,"How brain research can contribute to the evaluation of mathematical giftedness," *Psychological Assessment and Test Modeling* 55, no. 4 (2013): 415-437.

2. Jonathan Wai and Martha Putallaz, "The Flynn effect puzzle: A 30-year examination from the right tail of the ability distribution provides some missing pieces," *Intelligence* 39, no.6 (2011): 443–455, http://dx.doi.org/10.1016/j.intell.2011.07.006.

3. Gifted Development Center (website), The Columbus Group, http://www.gifteddevelopment.com/isad/columbus-group.

4. Aliza Alias, Saemah Rahman, Rosadah A. Majid, and Siti F.M. Yassin, "Dabrowski's overexcitabilities profile among gifted students," *Asian Social Science* 9, no.16 (2013): 120-125, https://doi.org/10.5539/ass.v9n16p120.

5. Altaras-Dimitrijević Ana, "A faceted eye on intellectual giftedness: Examining the personality of gifted students using FFM domains and facets," *Psihologija* 45, no. 3 (2012): 231-256.

6. Emily Kircher-Morris and Devon MacEachron, "Episode 27: Separating Truth From Mental Myths," March 6, 2019, *Mind Matters Podcast*, https://www.mindmatterspodcast.com/home/2019/3/6/episode-27-separating-truth-from-mental-myths.

7. Tamara Fisher, "Unwrapping the Gifted: What Brain Images Show Us About Gifted Learners," *Education Week Teacher* (blog), *Education Week*, February 9, 2010, http://blogs.edweek.org/teachers/unwrapping_the_gifted/2010/02/what_brain_imaging_shows_us_ab.html.

8. Li Zhang, John Q Gan and Haixian Wang, "Neurocognitive Mechanisms of Mathematical Giftedness: A Literature Review," *Applied Neuropsychology: Child* 6, no.1 (2017): 79-94, http://dx.doi.org/10.1080/21622965.2015.1119692.

9. Kun Ho Lee, Yu Yong Choi, Jeremy R. Gray, Sun Hee Cho, Jeong-Ho Chae, Seungheun Lee, and Kyungjin Kim, "Neural correlates of superior intelligence: Stronger recruitment of posterior parietal cortex," *NeuroImage* 29, no. 2 (January 2006): 578-586, http://dx.doi.org/10.1016/j.neuroimage.2005.07.036.

10. Rebecca Bull, Wendy A. Davidson, and Emily Nordmann, "Prenatal Testosterone, Visual-Spatial Memory, and Numerical Skills in Young Children," *Learning and Individual Differences* 20, no. 3 (June 2010): 246-250, http://dx.doi.org/10.1016/j.lindif.2009.12.002.

11. Jaroslava Durdiaková, Silvia Lakatošová, Aneta Kubranská, Jolana Laznibatová, Andrej Ficek, Daniela Ostatníková, and Peter Celec, "Mental rotation in intellectually gifted boys is affected by the androgen receptor CAG repeat polymorphism," *Neuropsychologia* 51, no. 9 (August 2013): 1693–1698.

12. Robert A. Hicks, and Christine M. Dusek, "The Handedness Distributions of Gifted and Non-Gifted Children, *Cortex* 16, no. 3 (October 1980): 479-481, http://dx.doi.org/10.1016/S0010-9452(80)80048-7.

13. Roberto Colom, Sherif Karama, Rex E. Jung, and Richard J. Haier, "Human Intelligence and Brain Networks," *Dialogues in Clinical Neuroscience* 12, no. 4 (December 2010): 489-501. https://www.ncbi.nlm.nih.gov/pmc/articles/PMC3181994/.

14. Arthur W. Toga and Paul M. Thompson, "Genetics of Brain Structure and Intelligence," *Annual Review of Neuroscience* 28 (2005): 1–23, http://dx.doi.org/10.1146/annurev.neuro.28.061604.135655.

15. Laura B. Perry, "Causes and Effects of School Socio-Economic Composition? A Review of the Literature," *Education and Society* 30, no. 1 (2012): 19-35, https://doi.org/10.7459/es/30.1.03.

16. Matthew T. McBee, Scott J. Peters, and Erin M. Miller, "The Impact of the Nomination Stage on Gifted Program Identification: A Comprehensive Psychometric Analysis," *Gifted Child Quarterly* 60, no. 4 (October 2016): 258-278, http://dx.doi.org/10.1177/0016986216656256.

17. Brooke N. Macnamara, David Moreau, and David Z. Hambrick, "The Relationship Between Deliberate Practice and Performance in Sports: A Meta-Analysis," *Perspectives on Psychological Science* 11, no. 3 (2016): 333-50, http://dx.doi.org/10.1177/1745691616635591.

18. Daniel Westreich, "Berkson's bias, selection bias, and missing data," *Epidemiology* 23, no. 1 (January 2012): 159-64, https://www.ncbi.nlm.nih.gov/pmc/articles/PMC3237868/.

19. James J. Lee, et al., "Gene discovery and polygenic prediction from a genome-wide association study of educational attainment in 1.1 million individuals", *Nature Genetics* 50, (July 23, 2018): 1112–1121, https://www.nature.com/articles/s41588-018-0147-3.

20. Andrew Van Dam, "It's better to be born rich than gifted," *Washington Post* October 9, 2018, https://www.washingtonpost.com/business/2018/10/09/its-better-be-born-rich-than-talented/

21. Thomas E Scruggs and Margo A. Mastropieri, "How gifted students learn: Implications from recent research," 6, no. 4 (1984): 183-185, http://dx.doi.org/10.1080/02783198409552804.

22. Jeff Guo, "These kids were geniuses—they were just too poor for anyone to discover them," *Washington Post*, September 22, 2015, https://www.washingtonpost.com/news/wonk/wp/2015/09/22/these-kids-were-geniuses-they-were-just-too-poor-for-anyone-to-discover-them/.

23. Margarita Bianco, "The Effects of Disability Labels on Special Education and General Education Teachers' Referrals for Gifted Programs," *Learning Disability Quarterly* 28, no. 4 (November 1, 2005): 285–293, http://dx.doi.org/10.2307/4126967.

24. Bernie Devlin, Stephen E. Fienberg, Daniel P. Resnick, and Kathryn Roeder, eds. *Intelligence, Genes, and Success: Scientists Respond to The Bell Curve*, (New York: Copernicus, 1997).

25. Ed Yong, "Chinese Project Probes the Genetics of Genius" *Nature*. (May 14, 2013), http://www.nature.com/news/chinese-project-probes-the-genetics-of-genius-1.12985.

26. Doresa Jennings, "Gifted Cubed – The Expanded Complexity of Race and Culture in Gifted and 2e Kids," *Global #GTCHAT Powered by TAGT*, (March 4 2015), https://globalgtchatpoweredbytagt.wordpress.com/2015/03/04/gifted-cubed-the-expanded-complexity-of-race-and-culture-in-gifted-and-2e-kids/.

27. Joy Lawson Davis, "3E: Gifted, Black and Having Special Academic and Behavioral Needs," *Teaching for High Potential* (Winter 2018), http://www.nagc.org/sites/default/files/Publication%20THP/THP_Winter_2018_SpecialPopulations.pdf.

28. Graham Chaffey, *Specialisation Module 4 — Part 1. Gifted and Talented Education, Professional Development Package for Teachers, Specialisation, Module 4.* (Sydney: GERRIC, University of NSW, 2004), 8-19.

29. David Lubinski, and Camilla P. Benbow, "Study of Mathematically Precocious Youth After 35 Years. Uncovering Antecedents for the Development of Math-Science Expertise," *Perspectives on Psychological Science* 1 (2006): 316-345, http://dx.doi.org/10.1111/j.1745-6916.2006.00019.x.

30. Nicholas Colangelo, Susan Assouline, and Miraca Gross, "A Nation Deceived: How Schools Hold Back America's Brightest Students, Volume II," *The Templeton National Report on Acceleration*, (Iowa City: The Connie Belin & Jacqueline N. Blank International Center for Gifted Education and Talent Development, 2004), 87-96.

31. Susan Assouline et al., *Iowa Acceleration Scale. A Guide for Whole-Grade Acceleration K-8*, 3rd ed. (Iowa City: Great Potential Press, 2009).

32. Martin Voracek, "National intelligence and suicide rate: an ecological study of 85 countries," *Personality and Individual Differences* 37, no. 3 (August 2004): 543–553, http://dx.doi.org/10.1016/j.paid.2003.09.025.

33. Ruth I. Karpinski et al., "High intelligence: A risk factor for psychological and physiological overexcitabilities," *Intelligence* 66 (January–February 2018): 8-23, https://doi.org/10.1016/j.intell.2017.09.001.

34. Dean K. Simonton, "Reverse engineering genius: historiometric studies of superlative talent," *Annals of the New York Academy of Sciences* 1377 (2016): 3-9, http://dx.doi.org/10.1111/nyas.13054.

35. Donna Y. Ford et al., "A Culturally Responsive Equity-Based Bill of Rights for Gifted Students of Color," *Forest of the Rain Production.* (March 2018), https://www.forestoftherain.net/donna-y-ford-kenneth-t-dickson-joy-lawson-davis-michelle-trotman-scott-and-tarek-c-grantham-a-culturally-responsive-equity-based-bill-of-rights-for-gifted-students-of-color-8203.html.

36. David Lubinski and Camilla P. Benbow, "Study of Mathematically Precocious Youth After 35 Years: Uncovering Antecedents for the Development of Math-Science Expertise," *Perspectives on Psychological Science* 1, no. 4, (2006): 316-345, http://dx.doi.org/10.1111/j.1745-6916.2006.00019.x.

37. Catherine Wormald, "Intellectually gifted students often have learning disabilities," *The Conversation* (March 25, 2015), http://theconversation.com/intellectually-gifted-students-often-have-learning-disabilities-37276.

38. Karen Rogers, "Worth the Effort: Finding and Supporting Twice Exceptional Learners in Schools," keynote speech, 22nd Biennial World Conference, World Council of Gifted and Talented Children, July 20, 2017, https://www.youtube.com/watch?v=U8aLf9TY97U.

39. Margarita Bianco, "The Effects of Disability Labels on Special Education and General Education Teachers' Referrals for Gifted Programs," *Learning Disability Quarterly* 28, no. 4 (November 2005): 285–293, http://dx.doi.org/10.2307/4126967.

40. Eric Michael Johnson, "The WEIRD Evolution of Human Psychology," *Scientific American*, December 7, 2011, https://blogs.scientificamerican.com/primate-diaries/the-weird-evolution-of-human-psychology/.

41. Henrich, Joseph, Steven Hein, and Ara Norenzayan, "The Weirdest People in the World?," *Behavioral and Brain Sciences* 33, no. 2-3 (2010): 61–83, http://dx.doi.org/10.1017/S0140525X0999152X.

42. Yee Han Chu and Bradley Myers, "When the world is just too rough: Twice exceptional gifted children with sensory processing disorder," speech, 22nd Biennial World Conference, World Council for Gifted and Talented Children, July 20, 2017, https://world-gifted.org/openconf/modules/request.php?module=oc_program&action=summary.php&id=165.

43. Karen Keppel, "*2e From an Eight Year Old's Perspective*" (blog), Leith Occupational Therapy, May 1, 2016, http://leithot.nz/2016/05/01/2e-from-an-eight-year-olds-perspective.html.

44. Henrietta Cook and Timna Jacks, "We don't want this to be a dirty little secret': The school ditching the ATAR," *The Age*, March 5, 2017, http://www.theage.com.au/victoria/we-dont-want-this-to-be-a-dirty-little-secret-the-school-ditching-the-atar-20170303-guqjbj.html.

45. Peter Grey, "A Survey of Grown Unschoolers I: Overview of Findings. Seventy-five unschooled adults report on their childhood and adult experiences," *Psychology Today*, June 7, 2014, https://www.psychologytoday.com/au/blog/freedom-learn/201406/survey-grown-unschoolers-i-overview-findings.

46. Wes Beach, *Self-Directed Learning: Documentation and Life Stories.* (Olympia: GHF Press, 2015), 25-42.

47. "Granny Cloud Teaching Children," Granny Cloud, last modified June 26, 2013, http://www.grannycloud.net/.

48. Jade Rivera, *Micro-Schools: Creating Personalized Learning on a Budget.* (Olympia: GHF Press, 2016), 16.

About the Author

Kathleen Humble is a gifted and 2e advocate and writer in Melbourne, Australia. She writes about her 2e family, which includes her very patient husband and their two homeschooled children, at Yellow Readis (www.yellowreadis.com). In her previous life, she was a mathematician, failed PhD student, computer programmer, and occasional puppeteer. She has written for numerous publications, including "The Mighty," and done many talks on educating gifted and twice-exceptional kids, including presenting at the 22nd Biennial World Conference on Gifted and Talented Children in Sydney in 2017. Kathleen was a Writers Victoria Write-ability Fellow in 2018. Occasionally, she dabbles with the idea that she's actually a real author.